Scammed By Society

The Contextual Theology and Christian Ethics of the Irish Travelers in the United States of America

Scammed By Society

The Contextual Theology and Christian Ethics of the Irish Travelers in the United States of America

A Moral Ethnographic Study

John M. Stygles

For My Parents

Preface

In this study the author explores the contextual theology and Christian ethics of a group of people living in the United States called "Irish Travelers". This study is partially an ethnographic study of a sub-culture of America as well as an exploration of the theology and ethics of a group considered by many Americans as "scammers and con-men".

Other studies have been conducted on the Irish Travelers yet this research explores their theology and ethics as interpreted by their worldview, or cultural logics. An unprecedented amount of access has been availed to the author over a three and a half year period. The result is a fresh and revealing look at a group of people and the actions they take to preserve their culture and traditions.

Contents

Acknowledgements

The author wishes to express sincere appreciation to The Irish Travelers, also known as "Mississippi Travelers," who trusted me enough to discuss some very personal details about the Traveler community. Without their confidence and assistance, this paper would not be possible.

To Dr. Peter R. Gathje, Professor Steven R. Edscorn and Memphis Theological Seminary for their assistance in the preparation of this thesis.

Special thanks is given to Kathryn Peirce and John Giantis for their editorial expertise. Finally, to M. D. Yander for the space and time needed to complete this work.

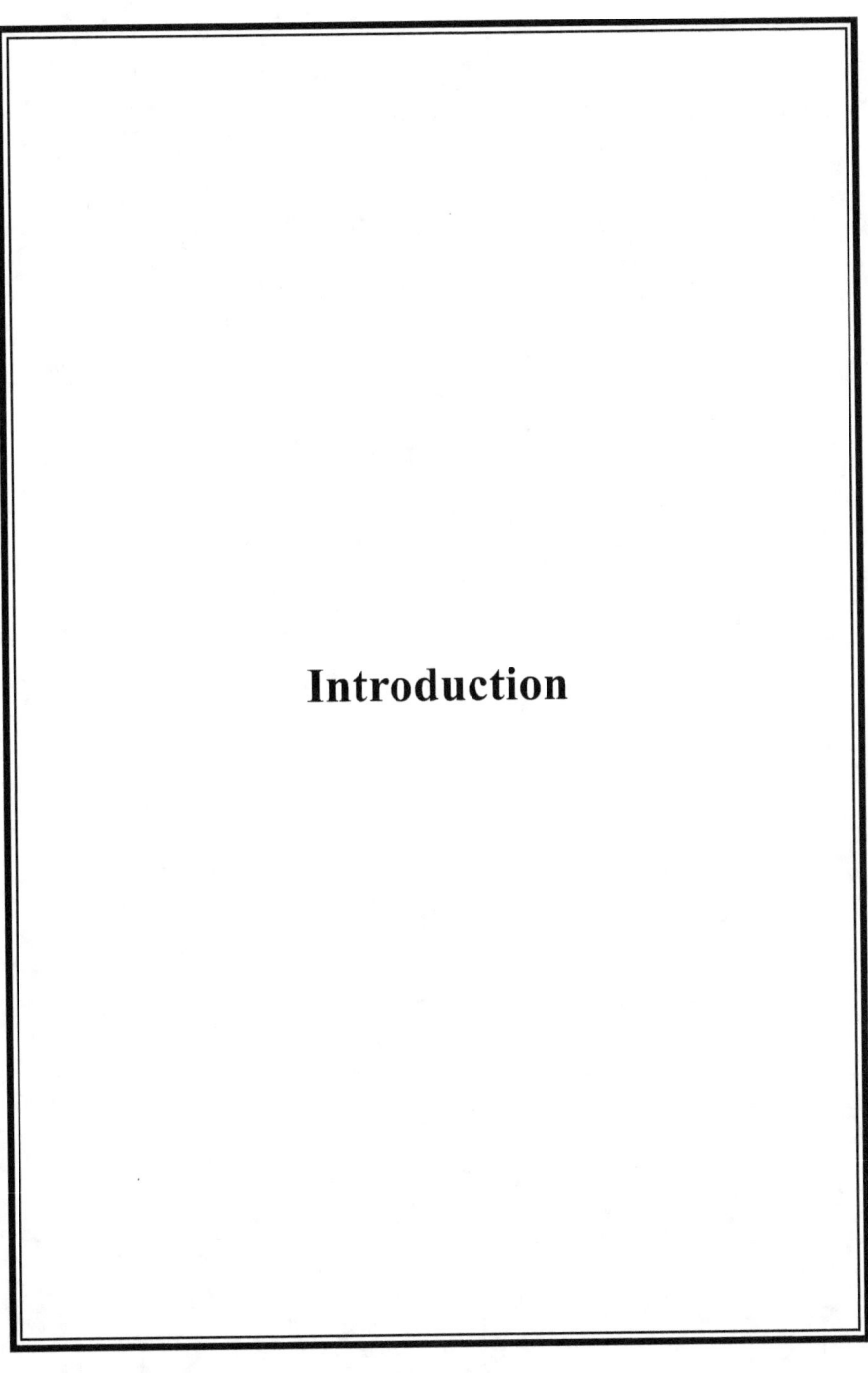

Introduction

It is sometimes surprising that in the year 2009 there could be a sub-culture of people in the United States of America of which very few Americans are aware. In September of 2002, most of America learned of this group of people known as the Irish Travelers via local television, newspapers and magazines.[1] This awareness came about as a result of a woman by the name of Madelyne Gorman Toogood being charged with abusing her daughter. Toogood was videotaped repeatedly slapping her daughter in the back seat of an SUV in a Kohl's department store parking lot in Mishawaka, Indiana.[2]

This event brought more attention upon the Irish Travelers in the United States than any other single event. One of the reasons the public does not hear about the Irish Travelers is that they maintain a low profile. They keep to themselves and have few, if any, relationships with non-Travelers.

Irish Travelers have made accommodations in blending with the general society. Although there is interaction with outsiders or non-Travelers, they have avoided assimilation, holding true to their traditions and culture.

Over the past three and a half years, I have observed and interacted with members of the Traveler community in Memphis, Tennessee. Prior to that direct involvement, I became aware of the Travelers by listening to stories told by my Mother and Aunts, who were first-generation Irish-Americans. Many of those stories are part

---

1   Transcript. "Interview With Don Wright - Kris Osborn CNN Anchor." *CNN SUNDAY*. 22 September 2002. 17 August 2008. http://transcripts.cnn.com/TRANSCRIPTS/0209/22/sun.04.htm

2   McGuire, John M. "Irish Travelers: Some Call Them Tight-Knit; Others Say They're Cons". St Louis Post-Dispatch (MO) (Sept 29, 2002): B1. Custom Newspapers. Gale. Memphis Theological Seminary. 9 Oct. 2008

of an oral history or tradition passed down through the generations; part is folklore, and part is creative exaggeration.

I have been fortunate and honored to be invited into the Traveler community because of my status as a priest in the United Catholic Church – an independent/Old Catholic faith community. I have learned a great deal about this group of Travelers; their culture and tradition. It is because of this exposure and involvement that I examined the public image versus the private communal image.

As a result of this thesis I hope to provide a better understanding of the contextual theology and ethics of the Irish Travelers and how they justify the scam. This moral ethnography is rooted in my understanding of interactions between the Travelers and those most likely to be affected by their actions.

In many respects this is an ethical case study, an internal analysis that holds a standard for the reflection and evaluation of the Travelers' "vision of life." It is the Travelers' vision of life which is embodied into practice and by extension into the life of the people to see how their moral life holds them together.

Clemens Sedmak states in *Doing Local Theology: A Guide for Artisans of a New Humanity,* "Cultures are expressions of our attempts to come to terms with life. Cultures express the human need for security and meaning and the human fear of chaos. Theology is about the whole human situation."[3] Sedmak provides one of the ways to approach the Irish Travelers and their culture.

When the Irish Travelers began to arrive in America during the mid-nineteenth century they had all of the expectations of their fellow Irish; to seek hope and opportunity. They ventured miles across the Atlantic seeking a way to keep their family fed and together. They carried their culture, religion and traditions with them and held on tightly. Yet, a century and a half later the Travelers

---

3   Sedmak, Clemens. *Doing Local Theology: A Guide for Artisians of a New Humanity.* Maryknoll: Orbis Books, 2007. P 74

have been referred to as "pariah group" and have been subjected to ridicule and scorn.[4]

Post-Famine life in Ireland was undoubtedly difficult. Yet, the Travellers of Ireland were conditioned to living a life with uncertainty.[5] The name given to this group of people is self-descriptive "Traveller". Their itinerant lifestyle had been their only way of earning a living, traveling from one town to another plying their trade.

The great exodus from Ireland to United States occurred during the 1840's. According to oral history the first Traveller to arrive in the United States was Tom Carroll.[6] Jared Harper documented statements of the Traveler oral history in this dissertation written in 1988. Harper wrote "Eventually, (Tom Carroll) saved enough money to send back to Ireland to bring his family over. He also sent for his best friend, Peter Sherlock."[7]

Several of my sources in the "Mississippi Traveler" community agree with that history although immigration records at Castle Garden in New York indicate many families with "Traveller" surnames arrived during between 1848 and 1885. A Thomas Carroll, age 27, did arrive in the United States on May 27, 1849 aboard the ship *Cambridge*.[8] I include this because in searching through the earliest records kept at Castle Garden, this Thomas Carroll is the

---

4   Greeley, Andrew M. "Irish Travelers - A Pariah People." 13 October 2002. TravellersRest. 18 August 2008. http://www.travellersrest.org/greeleypa-riah.htm. Originally published on http://www.southtownstar.com

5   Traveller: The spelling of Traveller with the double "L" is an Irish spelling. The "Travelers" in the United States have dropped the double-L. Any spelling of Traveller with the double-L is in referencing the Irish Travellers in Ireland.

6   Harper, Jared V. *The Irish Travelers of Georgia.* Thesis (Ph. D.)--University of Georgia, 1977, 1984. P30

7   Ibid.

8   (CastleGarden.Org) http://www.castlegarden.org. "America's First Immigration Center". 2005. Accessed 11/10/2008.

first individual to have listed "Tinker" as his occupation. This may be the "Tom Carroll" of which the Travelers refer.

"Tinker" is a term that was given to the Irish Travellers because of their trade in working with tin and repairing pots and pans. The term is considered derogatory and offensive by both the Travellers in Ireland and those living in United States today. The term "Tinker" identifying this group of people has been used in a negative manner for many years. Many mis-behaving children of Irish decent or heritage may have been told that "if you don't begin to behave, I'll sell you to the Tinkers."[9] Generations of Irish-Americans have perpetuated negative connotations and stereotypes of the Travelers through myths and folklore.

The story of Tom Carroll, which is so difficult to document, is similar to the stories of how the Irish Travellers came to exist. We know that a group's history is often documented through oral tradition. With Irish Travellers there appears to be many possible sources or beginnings for this group. People who are "un-settled" and travel from town to village can be considered travelers. What caused these people to become travelers might have been economic or a traditional way-of-life.

The Travellers who came to the United States have maintained their communities in a traditional manner that has become their way-of-life. The Travelers are a community of people that although not isolated from the rest of society, maintain customs and traditions that separate them from non-Travelers. In fact, the community today imparts a way of life that would be more common to the mid-nineteenth century, despite the use of modern conveniences such as automobiles, mobile technology and the internet. You would not find

---

9   "Sell you to the Tinkers": During my research I was reminded by more than one sibling or relative of this expression. In Irish-American culture there has always been myth and folklore associated with the Travellers in Ireland. Primarily negative sayings and symbols have been attached to this group of people, including that they will "steal your children".

Traveler communities in the United States increasing in numbers because of economics. Outsiders do not join the Travelers.

According to Harper, Tom Carroll became successful trading in horses and that led to sending money back to Ireland for his family and friends. Harper writes in his dissertation and this is corroborated by stories told to me that the first group of Travellers from Ireland included the following families: "The O'Hara, Riley's, McNamara's, Gorman's, Sherlock's, Carroll's, Costello's, and Daly's."[10] Of these families, I have interviewed or spoken with members of the Riley, Gorman, Sherlock, Carroll, and Costello families. There are other "family surnames" within the Traveler community, yet there are members of at least five of the original eight families living in the Memphis area.

The Travelers tend to raise their children in the Roman Catholic Church. This is a tradition carried over from their heritage in Ireland. How they view Roman Catholicism is open for interpretation. The women of the community practice their faith more openly through devotions and regular attendance at Mass. The men tend to be more introverted when it comes to faith practices.

Roman Catholicism provides its followers a solid foundation on which their faith is based. The practice of that faith can differ from community to community or culture to culture. It is upon that foundation that the Travelers practice their faith. Travelers express a tendency towards devotions and rituals more common to pre-Vatican II, yet involvement of Laity within the Church has expanded the options of practice for the Travelers and other Roman Catholics.

The men of the community are the providers. Today, as was the case when Travellers first came to United States, they tend to be independent business people. In many ways they express the "American Dream" with their entrepreneurial spirit, yet often their practices are called into question.

10   Harper, Jared V. *The Irish Travelers of Georgia*. Thesis (Ph. D.)--University of Georgia, 1977, 1984. P33

Originally, many of the Travelers were involved in horse and mule trading beginning with Tom Carroll. [11,12] Memphis became an important stop in the mule trading as this city was a center for auctions and trade. Trading in horses and mules not only takes knowledge of animals, a skill they brought over from Ireland and passed down, but the ability to communicate convincingly with those who are buyers.

Today, the Travelers would be considered semi-itinerants where the workers travel seasonally to earn a living and return to a settled community. This more sedentary lifestyle is partially the result of state government's assertion for compulsory school attendance for children. This accommodation has been made by the community with some risk to their ethnic and cultural identity.

11   Any early research on the Travelers will indicate this occupation. Much of what I will indicate in this paper is a result of interviews conducted with members of the Traveler community. Independent documentation can be found in the Harper dissertation.

12   Harper, Jared V. *The Irish Travelers of Georgia*. Thesis (Ph. D.)--University of Georgia, 1977, 1984. p 41ff

From Whence They Came

Many Irish-Americans can tell you what county their ancestors are from, some might even know the town or village, yet the Travellers have no roots in the country-side. In my discussions with the Travelers here in Memphis, not one could provide me with a county of origin. Living a nomadic lifestyle would cause this ambiguity.

There are a variety of reasons why this group of people became itinerants. Traditional crafts and skills is one of the primary reasons to adopt this way of life. Travellers have been known for their skills in working with tin and metal repair. In smaller towns and villages where there is not a constant source of pots and pans to be repaired, it would require frequent travel if one was to earn a sustainable income.

Their choice of wagon, or caravan, provided an identity for these people. The caravan's barrel-shaped design is similar to wagons used by Gypsies. This is one of the reasons Travellers in Ireland have been referred to as Gypsies. This mislabeling is common here in the United States as well.

As time progressed, these Travelers began to be identified not as individuals but as their own group. As groups became larger they would stand out from what is referred to as "settled people." Within these clusters of people a sense of community was formed that provided safety in their growing numbers. The Travellers also spoke their own language, referred to as Shelta or Cant.[13] This language is unique to the Travellers and is still used today.

Arranged marriages also became both a means of strengthening the group and insuring economic sustainability. It was not uncommon

---

13   Harper, Jared V. *The Irish Travelers of Georgia*. Thesis (Ph. D.)--University of Georgia, 1977, 1984 p25

for marriages in Ireland to be arranged even as late as the later part of the nineteenth century and early twentieth century. One exception to arranged marriages unique to the Travellers was that cousins could be betrothed to one another giving way to "endogamous marriages".[14] It was not only rare, but often forbidden, for a Traveller to marry someone from outside their community.

This practice of arranged marriage within the community was necessary as the family units played a major role in the economics and survival of the community as a whole. Skills were taught from father to son. Mother's taught their daughters not only the basics of maintaining a family unit such as childcare and cooking, but also their role in providing economically for the family.

When finances were slow it would not be uncommon to observe Traveller women with baby in tow seeking hand-outs at churches and pubs in Ireland.[15] This also added to the negative image of Travellers in general.

In addition to tinsmithing and repair, Travellers were also known for their ability to deal in horses.[16] Their skill in identifying a temporarily lame horse ready for successful rehabilitation was admirable. Often, their confidence in the knowledge of horses would put unsuspecting laypersons at a severe disadvantage. This skill of working with horses, combined with the charm common to many salespersons, was one of the main sources of gaining income for early Travelers.

Travellers in Ireland did what was necessary to put food on the table, from cleaning a chimney to fixing a roof. They were adaptable to their circumstances, and with skill and 'luck,' would convince "settled people" that they were able to repair anything.

---

14   Harper, Jared V. *The Irish Travelers of Georgia*. Thesis (Ph. D.)--University of Georgia, 1977, 1984.p3
15   Un-named Traveler. Personal Interview. November 2006
16   Harper, Jared V. *The Irish Travelers of Georgia*. Thesis (Ph. D.)--University of Georgia, 1977, 1984 p5

Over the years, the Travellers maintained the same routes along the roadways. They would be expected to arrive during certain times of the year and many "settled people" would have things for them to do when they arrived. Yet, upon completion of their projects and repairs; Travellers were also expected to "move on" as once they served their purpose of completing repairs they were not welcomed by the settled populations.[17]

Most Travellers in Ireland were baptized Roman Catholic. Because of their itinerant lifestyle, many failed to receive all of the Sacraments in a timely fashion because of lack of study and non-association with a Parish.[18] Travellers in Ireland may have been considered Roman Catholic by birth, but for the most part were non-practitioners.

In many ways the faith practices of the Travellers differed little from other Irish. Kirby Miller writes in *Emigrants and Exiles: Ireland and the Irish Exodus to North America*: "Pre Famine Catholics *were* devout, but their piety was expressed primarily in archaic, communal traditions which had originated in pre-Christian times and had since acquired only a thin veneer of medieval Catholicism."[19]

The Irish have commonly been known as storytellers and "having the gift of gab". Much of this perception comes from a tradition that is passed down through myths and folklore. The Irish story has many colors and textures; truth is sometimes mixed with fiction or just simply exaggerated. Oral history was the primary source of maintaining traditions and customs.

Much of the history of the Irish Travelers has not been documented except to include them in the general category of Irish-Americans, yet with the help of several Travelers living in Memphis, Tennessee, I have been able to construct a "reasonable"

---

17   Ibid. p7
18   Ibid. p21
19   Miller, Kerby A. *Emigrants and Exiles: Ireland and the Irish Exodus to North America*. New York: Oxford University Press, 1985. P. 73

oral history of events. I stress reasonable as I recognize that oral history is often told as seen through the "teller's" eyes. Therefore, wherever possible I have documented timelines and important facts with independently recorded history.

As previously mentioned, the name of "Tom Carroll" is thought to be the first Traveler to arrive in America. The time period for this ranges between 1840 and 1850 according to accounts passed down within the community. It is also agreed to that Carroll became successful in trading horses and that his or this trade as a source of income encouraged other Travellers in Ireland to emigrate.

After a period of time in the Northern states a warmer temperate climate was the motivating factor for the Travelers to move to the Southern United States. During the 1850s, the Travelers were living in wagons, caravans, and eventually tents. The trades and skills that provided them an income in Ireland were not as easily plied in the rural South. Travelers who learned how to trade mules and horses were able to provide an income for their families in that manner, while others would travel the back roads painting and repairing barns, farm houses, and performing odd jobs.

Trading of horses and mules became more lucrative and family activities were centered on those trading sites. Nashville, TN was one such location. Sometime, in the years surrounding the Civil War, Traveler families began to center their operations in Nashville, TN. Much of the horse trading conducted over the years took place in the Nashville – Murfreesboro area. A closer connection with the Roman Catholic Church was formed with the Travelers using Nashville, TN as their hub. In the late 1800s, a fourth Roman Catholic church was built in Nashville, named St. Patrick. According to their website:

> One unique aspect of the parish is its connection to the "Irish Travelers." This is a group of Irish immigrants of the mid-1800's who have not assimilated into the American population as other ethnic groups have done over the years. Instead, this group remains clannish [and] live an itinerant lifestyle. Over

the years, various families comprising the Irish Travelers would appear in the Nashville area to hold a common funeral for those who had died since the last gathering. Weddings and baptisms were performed as the gathering was equated to a family reunion. Times have changed and the Irish Travelers no longer roam the countryside by wagon but they will return at times to St. Patrick and renew their connection to the parish. The Irish Travelers have shown their appreciation for St. Patrick by donation of the Infant of Prague statue found in the Narthex and the statue of Our Lady of Perpetual Help.[20]

The statement on St. Patrick's website indicates how connected the Travelers were to the Church. The donation of statues depicting "Our Lady" and "the Infant of Prague" are indications of how these icons play an import role in the devotional life of the Traveler community.

For many years the Catholic Church, and especially the priest, played a very important role in the communications of the Travelers. Often mail would be sent to a Traveler in care of the priest or church. With Nashville acting as central hub, it allowed one area for communication, reunions, weddings and funerals.

Atlanta, Georgia also played an important role in early years of the Travelers in the United States. Monsignor Noel C. Burtenshaw wrote an article for the *Newspaper of the Catholic Diocese of Atlanta* stating:

> For many years April 28 was a most important date for these travellers. On that date they would gather at the Shrine of the Immaculate Conception in downtown Atlanta for their annual funeral service. Since they continued a set pilgrimage throughout the year, should a member of the clan die, the remains were sent to an Atlanta funeral home and kept until that April date. Then, like a swarming army, the clan would gather and all the caskets

---

20   St. Patrick Catholic Church."St. Patrick Catholic Church History". Accessed8June2008.http://www.stpatricksnashville.org/ParishHistory.html

would be brought to "The Immaculate" for the funeral mass. Often there were five or six caskets in the sanctuary on that day.

Burial would then take place at Oakland cemetery. The graves and the plots are there to be seen to this day.[21]

This information is consistent with the oral history told to me. Travelers would gather in April in Atlanta for funerals and then in May meet in Nashville for reunions with other Travelers. Although not as regular, Nashville still is a gathering point for Traveler reunions. According to one Traveler, the activities are informal, yet they provide an opportunity for many different Traveler families to meet and talk about life on the road and possible engagements. Because these reunions drew Travelers from all over the United States, marriage arrangements could take place with other Traveler families not living in their immediate community.[22]

Today, the Irish Travelers in the United States are clustered in three geographic locations. The "Georgia Travelers" are located in Murphy Village (Edgefield), South Carolina. The "Texas Travelers" are located in White Settlement, Texas.[23] The "Mississippi Travelers" are located primarily in Memphis, Tennessee.

In addition to these groups, there are other Travelers located in various regions of the country. These groups are named: "Western Travelers", "Northern Travelers", "Scots-Irish Travelers", "Williamson Travelers", "English Travelers", "Ohio Travelers" and simply "Travelers."[24] These groups are also itinerant workers, yet not all can be identified by an ethnic group or unique cultural identity.

---

21   Burtenshaw, Msgr. Noel C. "Irish Travelling People Last Of A Special Tribe" *The Georgia Bulletin - Online Edition*. 13 March 1986. 8 August 2008. http://www.georgiabulletin.org/local/1986/03/13/b/
22   Un-named Traveler. Personal Interview. November 2006
23   Riley, Amanda (South Carolina). "Unwanted Exposure". *Time in Partnership with CNN*. 7 October 2002 accessed 9 September 2008. http://www.time.com/time/0,8816,1003381,00.html
24   Wright, Don. *SCAM! Inside America's Con Artist Clans*. Elkhart, IN. Cottage Publications. 1996 p. 266

Understanding the Traveler Worldview

Devout Roman Catholics

To understand the Travelers and what makes them different, one must have an understanding of the Irish-Americans that immigrated to these shores prior to the masses of Travelers. The common heritage that these groups share helps define facets of Traveler culture, especially regarding how this group understands their religion and practices their faith.

There are, in many ways, very few differences between the ways most Irish Roman Catholics view and practice their faith when compared to the Traveler community. Kirby Miller writes:

> Scholars have argued that eighteenth and nineteenth century Irish Catholicism was strongly influenced by Augustinian and Jansenist traditions, which overemphasized man's sinful nature consequent on Adam's fall, severely limited the scope for self—regeneration through reason and 'good works,' and thus placed primary reliance on negative sanctions ("Thou shalt not...") and church-centered devotional practices and penances, rather than an ethical behavior, as a means of obtaining grace.[25]

As Roman Catholics, the "faithful" are taught to learn and follow the Catholic Catechism as this is the teaching of the Church. Within the Catechism, there are rules to be followed and punishment for those who do not follow the rules. Yet, as a means to receiving grace, the Roman Catholic Church created the Sacrament of Reconciliation where a person who breaks the rules, a sinner, has the opportunity to confess and do penance.

---

25   Miller, Kerby A. *Emigrants and Exiles: Ireland and the Irish Exodus to North America.* New York: Oxford University Press, 1985. p.117

It is through the Roman Catholic Church that one receives grace and salvation by adhering to the rules, receiving the Sacraments and participating in the life of the Church. From cradle to grave the Roman Catholic Church is always present for their faithful. The practice of Penance or Reconciliation is one way to not only ask for forgiveness but to receive "Absolution" for one's sins.

The rules of the Church have been laid out and it would not be the case where a Traveler tries to change the rules, but it would not be difficult to see how the Travelers will work around the rules, finding a loophole. An example of this can be seen in the ways the Travelers maintain their cultural traditions in regards to the marriage ceremony involving minors.

"Roman Catholicism has been the essence of Irish America"[26] states Lawrence J. McCaffrey in his book *Textures of Irish America*. He added, "Catholicism contradicts the values of assimilated Irish Americans."[27] When one thinks about what Roman Catholicism offers, one can see how there can be a conflict between American values and the Church.

The Roman Catholic parish offered Irish people, who were primarily from rural areas, a way to maintain their culture within a larger urban environment. For many working-class Irish-Americans, the Roman Catholic Church offered a social and political purpose beyond a religious one. The growth and prosperity of most Irish-Americans was built upon the relationships developed within these parishes and neighborhoods.

The Travelers on the other hand, although primarily Roman Catholic, provided their own insular community in order to maintain their cultural identity. Roman Catholicism was the foundation for the practice of their faith, yet their cultural identity was defined

---

26   McCaffrey, Lawrence John. *Textures of Irish America*. Syracuse, N.Y.: Syracuse University Press, 1992. P. 176
27   Ibid.

by more than their Irishness or relation to the traditional Catholic Church.

According to Miller, "much evidence indicates that, in contrast to the Protestants they encountered in Ireland and North America, the Catholic Irish were more communal than individualistic, more dependent than independent, more fatalistic than optimistic, more prone to accept conditions passively than to take initiatives for change, and more sensitive to the weight of tradition than to innovative possibilities for the future."[28]

Thus, if we observe and compare the habits and behaviors of Protestants to Catholics one would see these differences revealed on a theological level. One of the "Marks of the Church" is the proper administration of the Sacraments of which only an ordained member of the Clergy Deacon, Priest, or Bishop can perform.[29] Martin Luther's belief of a "Priesthood of all Believers" removed this requirement of the Church.[30] Therefore, one could see the need for a community or dependence upon a Church versus being on one's own.

If one also looks at the teachings of the Roman Catholic Church, one would understand that to be "prone to accept conditions passively than to take initiatives for change" is part of how dependent a believer in the Roman Catholic faith becomes, relying upon an approved Catechism and a structured Liturgy to inform and direct the faithful to accept a particular moral way of life.[31] Roman Catholics are reminded every time they enter a church of the sacrifice and suffering of Jesus Christ as depicted upon the cross.

---

28   Miller, Kerby A. *Emigrants and Exiles: Ireland and the Irish Exodus to North America*. New York: Oxford University Press, 1985.p.107

29   Gonzalez, Justo L. *Essential Thelological Terms*. Louisville, KY: Westminster John Knox Press. 2005. P106.

30   Ibid. p. 140

31   Miller, Kerby A. *Emigrants and Exiles: Ireland and the Irish Exodus to North America*. New York: Oxford University Press, 1985.p107

Tradition plays a major role in the life and worldview of the Travelers. The traditions and ritual provided by the Roman Catholic Church offer a sense of security, of continuity, of redemption and grace. Devotions and intercession of the Saints through prayer are another practice of Roman Catholics.

Today it would not be uncommon to see Traveler women at their parish church praying the Rosary or the Stations of the Cross. Novenas are a common devotional still practiced by the women of this community. One might also witness such devotions as praying on one's knees from the back of the church up to the altar.

Within the Irish Traveler community Mary, the Mother of God, takes on special significance. It is common to observe statues of Mary outside the mobile homes where the Travelers reside. Mary is also a common first name amongst Traveler women.

The devotion to the Blessed Mother goes beyond superficial worship. There is a clear identification and connection that Traveler women have with Mary. Mary is seen as the one who stayed with Jesus in good times and bad. Mary was the steadfast disciple of Christ, not only the first to believe, but also the first to know that her son was the Son of God.

"The Wedding at Cana" from John 2:11 is read at most Traveler weddings. In this scripture, we see Mary portrayed as a respectful, yet knowing woman who has such full faith in Jesus that after he hears her plea she knows that he will make things right. Traveler women relate to this image as a strong reminder of how they must practice the faith of their Church and what the results will be.

There is recognition among Traveler women, although they may not say it in this way, that they are broken individuals, sinners who need to get right with God through the Church and the Sacraments to be forgiven and receive God's sanctifying grace.

Travelers in general believe that prayer connects them to God. Although the women are more overt than the men, it is not unusual to find Rosary beads in the pocket of male Travelers. One Traveler shared with me a metal decade "Rosary ring" that he "picked up" at one of the churches he visited while on the road. He was sure to mention that he left a donation for the "ring". He wanted to reassure me his connection to the Church was more than casual.

Connection to the Church, specifically to a parish or a particular priest is something of which Travelers find comfort. In Memphis, there are several parishes where Travelers have been involved with both positive and negative outcomes. St. John Parish and School on Lamar Avenue in Memphis holds a strong connection for the Travelers, as does St. Paul Parish and School on Shelby Drive. Travelers have also been involved with St. Joseph Church on Neely and St. Ann Church on Highland Avenue.

St. John's Parish holds a special place with many older Travelers who went to school there and were married in the church. A special bond developed between the Travelers and Father James Pugh who was Pastor of St. John's prior to his transfer to The Church of Incarnation in Collierville, TN in 1980.[32] Fr. Pugh was then assigned with the task of establishing and growing The Church of Incarnation during the years of 1980 through 1987. There was a deep respect and loyalty of the Travelers to this priest.

According to The Church of Incarnation website "Father Pugh's friends, the Irish Travellers, came out and very generously supported the Bazaars while Father Pugh was our parish priest. Father was the spiritual advisor for the Irish Travellers in Memphis."[33]

Four years after his arrival in Collierville, Father Pugh was able to raise a significant amount of money to build a church. Again, the Church website documents:

> The church was a blessing but brought with it several significant expenses, namely a large note, insurance payments and utility

---

32   Masserano, Judy and John & Goodin, Vicky. Catholic Church of The Incarnation. "The History of the Church of Incarnation-A Story of Love, Hope and Faith" © 2005. Accessed 8 August 2008

33   Ibid.

bills. Father Pugh told the parishioners they would need to give more in the collection or the heat would be turned off. Father Pugh called upon the Irish Travellers once again. They began coming to mass and donating to our collections which helped meet expenses until the parish membership grew large enough to cover our expenses.[34]

Several Travelers expressed that they have not attended The Church of Incarnation since Father Pugh's departure in 1987, because of the distance from their homes and the lack of hospitality.[35] Travelers have a strong sense of loyalty and take special pride in their relationship with priest and parish. Their appreciation is expressed through their generosity.

The Georgia Travelers showed an example of their loyalty and connection with a priest during the mid 1960's when "more than three hundred Irish Traveler families [...] settled on a fifty-acre parcel of land that they called Murphy Village. They [the Travelers] named the site for Father Joseph Murphy, a parish priest and advocate who started the settlement for Travelers and guided it for twenty years before his transfer in 1968."[36]

Another mention of Traveler gratitude is published on the Saint Patrick Roman Catholic Church of Nashville, TN website. It states:

> Times have changed and the Irish Travelers no longer roam the countryside by wagon but they will return at times to St. Patrick and renew their connection to the parish. The Irish Travelers have shown their appreciation for St. Patrick by donation of the Infant of Prague statue found in the Narthex and the statue of Our Lady of Perpetual Help.[37]

---

34   Ibid.

35   Ibid.

36   Casey, Dan and Conor. "Irish Travelers of Aiken County". Irish America Magazine. Sept./Oct. 1994. P.44-47

37   St. Patrick Catholic Church. "St. Patrick Catholic Church History". Accessed 8 June 2008. http://www.stpatricksnashville.org/ParishHistory.html

Generosity, especially to the Church, takes on an additional significance. Travelers believe that doing good works is important, especially for the Church. The Saint Patrick Catholic Church website also contains the history of the Infant of Prague statue:

> The origin of the miraculous statue of the Infant of Prague is shrouded in legend. It is known, however, that it was brought from Spain to Prague in the 16th century and enshrined there in Our Lady of Victory Church in 1628. Following a destructive invasion of the city and the church by the Turks, Father Cyril, one of the shrine's friars, was spoken to by the infant Jesus who encouraged him to repair the broken hands of this statue, promising "The more you honor me, the more I will bless you."[38]

The Travelers understand this quote as a teaching or lesson to be followed, "The more you honor me, the more I will bless you."[39] How better to honor a church than to not only provide for its upkeep but to add to the devotional icons. Just as Confession and Penance provide Absolution, it is believed gifts and good works also put one in good stead.

In June of 1996, the *Cincinnati Post* reported an arrest of a 15-year old boy who was part of a branch of the Irish Travelers. The boy, Edward Thomas Judd Burke, stated:

> He is a devout Roman Catholic who attends Mass each week, prays the Rosary and reads the Bible every day. But he acknowledges that he's also been driving on a phony driver's license for years and pulls scams like other Travelers. He sees no conflict between his religion and his lifestyle, saying he's been taught that God will forgive the Travelers.

---

38   St. Patrick Catholic Church. "History of the Infant of Prague". Accessed 8 June 2008. http://www.stpatricksnashville.org/InfantOfPragueStatue.html

39   Ibid.

God has given them "the right to do whatever we want and be free,"[40] he told the *Courier-Journal* this week during an interview at the Jefferson County Youth Center.[41]

This youthful explanation of what it means to be a Roman Catholic is not shared by all Travelers, nor do Travelers believe they are blessed and have a right to do whatever they want. But there is a sense amongst Travelers that they are different than other people because of their background and traditions which they have maintained by not intermingling with non-Travelers.

Father Joseph Murphy, referenced above was revered by the Travelers who lived in Georgia. Today, Travelers in Memphis, who knew Father Murphy personally, told me that this priest truly understood what it meant to be a Traveler. One Traveler stated that Father Murphy believed moving to Murphy Village would help the Travelers stay together. Another Traveler thought Father Murphy *sold them a bill of goods.*[42]

---

40   Edward Thomas Judd Burke: In an interview with one of the Mississippi Travelers, I was told that "the Burke's are not one of us." The reference was not necessarily to disassociate Burke as a Traveler, but not of their group. As mentioned previously, the Irish Travelers are primarily represented by three groups: Georgia Travelers, Mississippi Travelers, and Texas or Greenhorn Travelers. Other groups are usually a representation of Northern Travelers, Ohio Travelers, Scot-Irish Travelers, English Travelers and the like.
In the book *Scam,* by Don Wright the key character is a James Burke who is associated with the Northern Travelers although he does have some contact with the Georgia Travelers.
41   "Violence Breaks Silence Teen-Age Con Artist Talks After Pal Hurts Deaf Mute". *The Cincinnati Post* (Cincinnati, OH) (June 7, 1996): 16A. Custom Newspapers. Gale. Memphis Theological Seminary. 9 Oct. 2008
42   Father Murphy: Most of my interviews took place with Travelers in the "Mississippi" branch in Memphis, TN. There are family connections between the Mississippi Travelers and the Georgia Travelers and throughout the years marriages have been arranged bringing these groups even closer. Some of the Travelers interviewed in Memphis concerning Murphy Village and Fr. Murphy believe that, although well-intentioned, the Catholic Church has tried to control many social and cultural norms of the Travelers living within that parish.

Respect and loyalty are important to the Travelers and they will often rely on their priest for counsel and advice. Prior to the great potato famine and the mass emigration from Ireland in the 1840s, many Irish regarded the priest as being on top of the preverbal pedestal. This image of the priest being "above" the rest was not discouraged by the Roman Catholic Church.

In fact, the role of the priest as the one who administers the Sacraments, hears confessions, and grants Absolution in lieu of Christ promotes the priest's role and position in society. While this attitude and perception has been modified a great deal by better informed and well-educated parishioners today, according to Kirby Miller, author of *Emigrants and Exiles: Ireland and the Irish Exodus to North America,* in the mid-nineteenth century "priests were venerated largely because of purported magical powers to cure sickness, combat witches and fairies, and shield people from persecution and oppression."[43]

Kim Ablon Whitney, author of *See You Down The Road,* provides an interesting insight into the Travelers using the character *Big Jim.* In this fictional account, Big Jim and three other younger Travelers have just finished preparation for a "major scam." Big Jim has gathered his younger Travelers and reviewed the plan. Whitney writes:

> "I guess Big Jim decided he'd scared us enough because he stood up and announced, 'All right, let's go. There's someone we gotta talk to before we get this thing started.'"

> "Who?" Jimmy asked

> "God," Big Jim replied. "If you want a job to go well, you gotto pray to the big guy."[44]

---

43   Miller, Kerby A. *Emigrants and Exiles: Ireland and the Irish Exodus to North America.* New York: Oxford University Press, 1985. p.73
44   Whitney, Kim Ablon. *See You Down The Road.* New York. Dell Laurel-Leaf/Random House. 2004 p. 125

So Big Jim and the three others get on the road and seeing some people on the sidewalk ask directions to a church. They find a church although it is a non-Catholic church. They enter and are told by a cleaning woman that the church does not hold a Mass but a Service. This doesn't stop them as they continue down the aisle to a pew, get down on their knees and pray even though there is no kneeler. [45]

I interviewed Ms. Whitney about how she developed the character and she responded, "In crafting Big Jim's character I felt he wouldn't be concerned with or limited by ideas of who can worship where. In my mind, Big Jim would have gone to Temple if that was all that was around! To him it's all about being true to yourself and your beliefs, not sticking to societal rules."[46]

Traveler men, because they are on the road a majority of the time, are not as connected to their parish as are the women of the community. The practice of the Roman Catholic faith is a formality according to several Traveler men. These men expressed that devotions and faith in God tends to be more spiritual. They recognize and value the Sacraments of the Roman Catholic Church but rely on their personal connection to God.

As stated, women are the ones who insure the continuance of religious instruction and participation in the Roman Catholic Church. The education of children continues to be the responsibility of Traveler women but now, primarily due to the enforcement of truancy laws, most Traveler children attend parochial school.

Dr. Mary E. Andereck author of *Ethnic Awareness and the School: An Ethnographic Study*, based this book on her doctoral dissertation that she conducted in one of the Roman Catholic elementary schools in Memphis, TN. Dr. Andereck writes:

---

45   Whitney, Kim Ablon. *See You Down The Road*. New York. Dell Laurel-Leaf/Random House. 2004 p. 125
46   Stygles, John M. "Hello I have questions" "Finally Answers". E-mail to Kim Ablon Whitney. 21 September 2008

The Catholic school prepares its students for first communion in religion classes during the school day and, as a class, the children take first communion during one of the Sunday masses. Travelers, however have chosen to have their own first communion service, even if some of the children are attending the Catholic school and its preparatory classes.[47]

Once again, in order to maintain their traditions and cultural practices as Dr. Andereck stated, a separate communion service is conducted exclusively for the Travelers. There are many reasons for this separate celebration, nothing of which has to do with the sanctity of the Sacrament. The celebration of a child's First Holy Communion is a rite or ritual that is to be a community event.

Not only does the first communion act as a religious event, it also serves as an important social event for the Travelers. It is traditional for boys and girls to wear all white outfits, as an outward sign of their purity from sin, however Traveler children go to the extreme. Andereck writes, "Traveler girls wear long white, altered wedding gowns, with veils and trains, usually ordered out of Chicago for $200 to $400."[48]

One Traveler woman told me during a wedding that the dress that was being worn by the bride would be worn by her daughter when she received her first communion.[49] Great pride was expressed not for the frugality of saving the expense of a dress, but that her child was chosen to wear this very exclusive wedding dress on the day she receives her first communion.

Since many Traveler parents remove their children from school after the seventh or eighth grade, the preparation for Confirmation is conducted in the evening through the parish Confirmation classes.[50]

---

47   Andereck, Mary E. *Ethnic Awareness and the School: An Ethnographic Study*. Newbury Park, CA: SAGE Publications, Inc. 1992. P.31

48   Ibid. pages 31-32

49   Un-named Traveler. Personal Interview. 19 November 2008

50   Andereck, Mary E. Ethnic Awareness and the School: An Ethnographic Study. Newbury Park, CA: SAGE Publications, Inc. 1992. P.32

During the process of preparing for Confirmation, the child will choose a sponsor and select a Confirmation name. Selecting the name of a patron saint encourages the child to use their talents and gifts for the glory of God, in service to others. Usually the name chosen has relevance to the child. Andereck, who did her study in the late 1980's, noticed that boys tended to choose the name Jude and the girls chose Anne.[51] Today, the name "Seelos" has become common due to the reputation of Blessed Fr. Francis Xavier Seelos and his reported miracles.[52]

---

51   Ibid.
52   Information on Blessed Father Francis Xavier Seelos can be found on the Internet at http://www.seelos.org/

Marriage Rituals

Before we begin the exercise of examining the marriage practices and rituals of the Irish Travelers let us review what the common practices were in Ireland in the 1840's. Lawrence McCaffrey writes:

> Irish marriages were negotiated matches rather than romantic responses to passion and usually wives were much younger than husbands so love and strong sexual desire were not significant aspects of Irish family life. Catholic condemnations of premarital sex and urgings to avoid sin reinforced more that they generated Irish puritanism. Catholic teachings helped provide the strength to endure the physical and psychological torments of sexual abstinence and solitary living.[53]

McCaffrey continues:

> Parents raised most of their children for export. Surplus sons who could not inherit the farm or shop or secure jobs as tradesmen, or did not want to enter the church or become soldiers or policemen, and daughters without dowries for marriage or religious vocations or unable or unwilling to become servants in the big houses left for the United States.[54]

The picture of Irish life, marriage rituals, and customs would appear bleak compared to contemporary times. Many discussions took place with the Travelers concerning the marriage practices of their community. Before describing the current practices there are certain conclusions that can be made for how the Irish in general saw marriage. Just reviewing the statements made above which are based upon research conducted by Lawrence McCaffrey, one might perceive the following:

---

53   Ibid. p. 57
54   McCaffrey, Lawrence John. *Textures of Irish America*. Syracuse, N.Y.: Syracuse University Press, 1992.P. 12

1. In the 1840's the economy of Ireland was desperate with little opportunity.

2. Things were so bad that if a grown child did not have a skill, or desire to enter religious life, their only option was to emigrate to North America or another country.

3. Irish marriages were negotiated.

4. It was a custom within arranged (negotiated) marriages that the bride was younger than the groom.

5. Because of Catholic teachings on premarital sex, many couples were married at a young age.

6. The arrangements, or negotiations of marriages, were one of economics and not necessarily one of romance.

For many reasons today, discussing marriage and marriage arrangements with non-Travelers can be uncomfortable. Most non-Travelers bring to the discussion preconceived opinions based on contemporary American culture and norms. The Roman Catholic Church, via Diocesan rules and regulations, has imposed a moral imperative to Traveler traditions regarding marriage.

State governments have gone so far as to change laws involving minimum age requirements in response to pressure from well-meaning outsiders. In 1997, South Carolina Governor David Beasley signed into law a bill that "raised the bar on the legal age for marriages to 14 years for girls and 16 for boys."[55] According to reporting done by Kathy Steele of the *Augusta Chronicle*, this action was taken in "in response to reports that girls as young as 12 were being forced into arranged marriages with older men in the Irish Traveler community in Murphy Village."[56]

---

55   Steele, Kathy. "State Legal Marriage Age Raised". *The Augusta Chronical Online.* 13 June 1997 accessed 7 August 2008 http://chronicle.augusta.com/stories/061397/met_travelermarriage.html
56   Ibid.

Understanding this negative attitude and opinion towards what has been a part of the Irish Traveler culture and tradition for many years; one might be able to understand the reluctance of Travelers to enter into discussions with non-Travelers about this practice. The proliferation of negative publicity, articles and news stories concerning what is thought to be the Irish Traveler marriage practices has produced a "knee-jerk" reaction from politicians and well-intended individuals to impose their societal views, norms and mores over a tradition without first seeking the understanding of actual marriage practices.

For example, the actions taken by Governor David Beasley of South Carolina took place after "[a]n episode of *Dateline NBC* prompted public outcry, followed by a decision from Attorney General Charlie Condon to form the South Carolina Traveler Crime Task Force."[57]

Much of what was portrayed as marriage rituals was incorrect, according to one Traveler interviewed. This Traveler stated, "What was shown on television to be a procession of young girls being selected as potential future brides was actually little girls in their "First Communion" dresses."[58]

Pressure was placed upon the Irish Travelers living in Murphy Village, South Carolina as a result of this episode and the formation of the "South Carolina Traveler Crime Task Force". Kathy Steele of the *Augusta Chronicle* reported in March of 1997 that, "The program [*Dateline NBC*] spotlighted the tradition of arranged marriages in the community, and questioned whether Travelers allowed children under age 14 to marry - a violation of state law."[59]

---

57   Ibid.

58   Un-named Traveler. Personal Interview. 1 December 2008

59   Steele, Kathy. "Irish Travelers raided on fraud, other charges". *The Augusta Chronical Online.* 16 March 1997 accessed 8 August 2008 http://chronicle.augusta.com/stories/031697/met_murphy.html

As a result of the *Dateline NBC* story there was a raid on the Irish Traveler community of Murphy Village. Authorities were searching for the existence of under-age marriages among the Travelers. Kathy Steele writes:

> Aiken County Sheriff Howard said the task force investigated allegations of under-age marriages and were prepared to serve warrants. However, on advice from the attorney general's office, they were not made.

> ``That was disappointing to us because it was one of the driving forces in putting the task force together,'' the sheriff said. ``We really did address that issue. We had cooperation with other authorities and offices to look at ways to document under-age marriages. The issue is the ability to sustain a charge that would stick.''[60]

Once again, perception did not match reality. Many Travelers recount these raids as a form of persecution. One could argue that the failure "to serve warrants. [...], on advice from the attorney general's office," was an indication that the allegations of under-aged marriages was not substantiated.[61]

This background is provided in an attempt to allow the reader to understand the sensitivity of this matter. Irish Travelers maintain a cultural tradition that has since been lost or forgotten by most Irish-Americans. It was not uncommon for marriages to be arranged by family members in "the old Country," or Ireland." Marriages were also a business contract in many ways, based upon economics. As mentioned above, the bride was usually younger than the groom. This is partially because an older 'man' would have had the time to build some savings, learn a trade or establish a business. Also a dowry was usually part of the marriage contract. A majority of Americans in contemporary times do not hold true to these traditions and instead marry based on the idea of romantic love.

---

60   Ibid.
61   Ibid.

During the planning of one wedding in the Traveler community in Memphis, Tennessee, I had the opportunity to speak with the parents of both the bride and groom. The groom was a 22 year old man who was living with his parents when not on the road working. The bride was a 15 year old woman, who also lived with her parents. Both had been baptized in the Roman Catholic Church and received the Sacraments of Reconciliation, Holy Communion and Confirmation.

The parents and couple desired a church wedding but, because of rules set by the local Diocese, the Roman Catholic priest was prohibited from conveying the Sacrament of Marriage upon this couple. The parents and couple wanted this marriage blessed and sought another avenue.

One of the parents provided me with the back-story on this "coupling." Both families live in the same community and had known each other for many years. The parents get along well with each other in business and socially. In the years prior to the date of the wedding both sets of parents had discussed their children and what they felt would be a good "match or arrangement."

It is not only important for families to be concerned about the compatibility of the wedding couple, but they also take into account how this marriage will affect the extended family and community. What was emphasized to me was the freedom the bride-to-be or the groom-to-be had to veto this arrangement.[62]

The terms of the arrangement were not discussed with me, yet a dowry was mentioned as part of the agreement between families. Often, the groom-to-be will work with the father of the bride-to-be

---

[62]   The emphasis on the bride-to-be and the groom-to-be having freedom to choose not to participate in a marriage arrangement was stressed to me during this interview session and also by other Traveler parents of wedding couples I have met. I do believe this is true, but I would say the enculturation of children into the traditional values and norms is so strong, the option to choose and say no, just doesn't happen very often.

in order for the father to better know the groom-to-be and to help them build a financial nest-egg.

The age of the bride-to-be was brought up by the groom-to-be's father and he stated that it was tradition in the community to arrange marriages this way. He pointed out that twenty-three years prior to this event when he and his wife married she was only fourteen. He said, "...and we're still together, which is more than I can say for some other couples."[63]

It was explained that the couple would be married in a civil ceremony by a Judge when they went for the marriage license. In the State of Tennessee a young person can be married, with the parent's permission, at the age of fourteen. It is common practice that when the Judge grants this permission to obtain a marriage license the Judge will perform the marriage ceremony.

What was and is important to Traveler families is the blessing of the marriage. Since the Roman Catholic Church prevents one of their priests or deacons from administering the Sacrament or even blessing the marriage, the Travelers have gone outside of the church for an ordained minister to perform the ceremony.

As an Independent/Old Catholic Priest, I have been asked to bless these marriages since 2006. [64] The rites and rituals are the same as with the Roman Catholic Church, but the administration of the Sacrament of Matrimony is not "legal" in their eyes.

As a bit of irony, although the Roman Catholic Church will not allow a priest or deacon to perform the marriage ceremony they

---

63   Un-named Traveler. Personal Interview. November 2006

64   Independent/Old Catholic: The Old Catholic Church is the result of a schism that occurred in 1870 within the Roman Catholic Church over "papal infallibility". This action took place during Vatican I. Independent/Old Catholic Churches are not in Communion with the Roman Catholic Church yet both are Catholic in two distinct way: Apostolic Succession and belief in the Real Presence of Christ in the Eucharist. These denominations are frequently referred to as part of the "Independent Sacramental Movement".

do allow churches to be rented out for the wedding ceremony. In all appearances, a wedding ceremony officiated by a non-Roman Catholic priest looks no different than one done by a Roman Catholic priest.

Appearances are important to the Travelers in regards to marriage arrangements. Within a community, families know one another and if an arrangement is made between certain families, especially if one of those families is extremely *well-off*, then that arrangement may seem like a coup. If the intention is to find a good provider for your daughter, then the value of the arrangement becomes even more important.

Again, economics is a major factor in the marriage arrangements and agreements. This is not seen as being non-romantic, but realistic. The wedding couple will have responsibilities beyond their own family once married. Part of that is what maintains the traditions and customs. These are values that are taught at an early age, preparing Traveler children for the future.

This adherence to tradition and culture appears extremely patriarchal yet as one begins to better understand the Traveler culture, one finds an equal sharing of responsibilities between male and female. What may appear to non-Travelers as an oppressive system evolves into one that is based in love and provides power and justice for all members of the community.

Because of the iterant lifestyle of Traveler men, weddings are scheduled around the holidays of Thanksgiving, Christmas and New Years. Occasionally a wedding will be held at other times when the majority of the men are at their home base.

A wedding is very much a community event. Because it is the norm for weddings to occur during certain times of the years, formal invitations are not necessarily handed out or mailed to other members of the community. The mother-of-the-bride is usually in charge of preparing and organizing the wedding. Various tasks will be divided amongst siblings and other members of the community.

The wedding ceremony customarily takes place in the evening. It is not uncommon for the priest or minister and any other support people, such as photographers, video camera operators, organist and singers, to be at the church at the stated time only to wait up to five hours before the ceremony begins. Punctuality is not important. The start of the wedding begins once the bride is ready and notification is made via the telephone to the community. When the majority of the community has arrived the wedding procession begins.

The ritual of the wedding ceremony begins with the groom and his best man walking down the aisle. After the parents have been escorted down the aisle, the community procession begins. This includes other newlyweds, recently married couples especially if there are babies to show off. Then other younger Travelers boys and girls process, many of the young girls dressed in a fashion appropriate for a pageant. This is truly a community event, which embodies the spirit of fun and celebration.

The immediate wedding party is relatively small. This includes the bride and her maid-of-honor, the groom and his best man. The best man is often one of the eligible bachelors of the same age. The maid-of-honor is usually a younger child, often between the ages of six and ten years old.

Marriage to non-Travelers is not encouraged, and it is in fact discouraged. Any association with a non-Traveler for anything other than business is discouraged. The few exceptions to this rule would be for priests and nuns. Associating with a non-Traveler on a personal basis could ostracize that Traveler from the rest of the community.[65]

Divorce is extremely rare among Travelers both because of their deep devotion to the Roman Catholic Church and also due to the marriage arrangement between families. There are certain things that "will not fly", according to one Traveler woman. "We will not allow our daughters to be abused." She continued, "The families

---

65   Un-named Traveler. Personal Interview. November 2006

are too together and everyone knows what's happening with one another. The woman talk, the men talk. If a man gets out of hand one of the men will speak to him."[66]

In cases where divorce does occur, the wife and/or husband will plead their case through the Diocesan Tribunal prior to remarrying. It is important to maintain the connection to the Roman Catholic Church according to this Traveler. Divorce within a Traveler marriage is wholeheartedly discouraged by the Traveler community.

Marriages between Travelers and non-Travelers, when they occur are usually not supported by the community according to one Traveler who stated, "If they get divorced there may be an opportunity to reacquaint the Traveler with the community once again."[67]

66   Un-named Traveler. Telephone Interview. 12 December 2008
67   Un-named Traveler. Personal Interview. 3 January 2009

Family Life

Oral history tells us that after the first few families came to the United States of America, after the Famine and prior to the Civil War, "word and money" was sent to Ireland to bring additional family members; brothers, sisters, mothers, fathers, wives, cousins.[68] The opportunity that existed in America was the same for the Travelers as it was for the million other Irish that immigrated.

As previously described, the family unit is not only an association of blood relatives; it is a vital core of the economy of the Traveler community. Just as marriages are arranged based on what will be the best for the betrothed's financial security and development of a family; so too are families looking out for their later years.

There are three major clusters of Irish Travelers in the United States; Murphy Village, South Carolina where the group known as the Georgia Travelers have resided since the mid-1960's, White Settlement, Texas where the Texas Travelers established roots in the 1970's and Memphis, Tennessee where the Mississippi Travelers are based.[69]

The majority of Travelers known as Mississippi Travelers, hold residences in two different trailer parks in Memphis, Tennessee, although some do own "stick-built" homes in North-West Mississippi. There are approximately two-hundred and forty-seven families in the Memphis area according to one Traveler.[70] Living in a trailer park is their choice. It is a way of maintaining the traditional ties to the itinerant life and their culture.

One would be surprised when visiting one of these trailer homes as the only thing that indicates that these homes are mobile is the wheels underneath the structure. The furnishings, decorations, and electronics suggest the person living there is a person of means.

---

68   Un-named Traveler. Personal Interview. November 2006
69   Ibid.
70   Ibid.

Just as in Ireland, adult children live with their parents until they marry. Parents, grandparents, aunts and uncles all maintain separate residences even as they get older unless one becomes unable to care for themselves. Older members of the community are very much respected for their age, wisdom and experience. They ensure and guide the younger generations in ways to maintain the traditions and culture.

Young girls are taught from an early age their "traditional role" as mother, wife, and care-giver. Boys will work alongside their father and uncles learning a craft and developing skills that will allow them to provide for their family when they are ready to marry. These roles are very "old-fashioned" and traditional compared to contemporary societal life, but this is part of their culture.

Once again, appearances are deceiving as what "traditional role" means in this community. Along with maintaining a family and home comes the responsibility of managing money. I have been told by several Travelers both male and female that one of the responsibilities of the wives is to manage the money their husbands earn. This includes everything from managing investments to planning for health care and retirement along with maintaining a home. In contemporary society where money equals power, this elevates the role of the women of this community.[71]

Mary E. Andereck compared the role of Irish Traveler mothers to the role of school teachers and noted, "Their group membership is even more important to them because they will teach Traveler norms and values to their children."[72] Each generation passes on these traditions. School can be a problem for Traveler parents who are concerned with outside influences from their child's classmates. Socialization is discouraged outside the classroom.

---

71   Un-named Travelers. Personal Interviews. November 19 – 26, 2008
72   Andereck, Mary E. *Ethnic Awareness and the School: An Ethnographic Study*. Newbury Park, CA: SAGE Publications, Inc. 1992. P.64

One Traveler told me simply, "We take care of our own."[73] He went on to explain that "it's like a "neighborhood watch" where we take care of one another. There is never any trouble here, and if there was, we take care of our own."[74]

Amanda Ripley a writer for *Time.Com* interviewed Jim (Penn) Sherlock of Murphy Village in October of 2002 in response to the Madelyne Toogood incident. He was provided an opportunity to explain his view on Traveler family life. Sherlock stated: "we don't put our old folks in rest homes. We don't have as many divorces. And when a woman gets raped or a bank gets robbed, law enforcement doesn't come to Murphy Village."[75]

Newsweek updated their reporting of the 2002 Toogood case in 2007 quoting Joe Livingston, a senior agent with the South Carolina Law Enforcement Division: "It is an aberration of the normal Traveler behavior as far as hitting children and such; they really hold their children in high esteem and family has a high importance in their lives."[76]

Livingston has described the Traveler community and the way they live as a "paradox."[77] This is a common observation whether one is referring to the Georgia, Mississippi, or Texas Travelers.

My personal observations have shown me that family and community are all essential, the top priority for Travelers. There was an occasion when I was called upon to bless the marriage of a

---

73   Un-named Traveler. Personal Interview. 14 November 2007
74   Ibid.
75   Riley, Amanda (South Carolina). "Unwanted Exposure". *Time in Partnership with CNN*. 7 October 2002 accessed 9 September 2008. http://www.time.com/time/0,8816,1003381,00.html
76   Newsweek Web Exclusive. "Seriously Prejudiced: Madelyne Toogood's Ethnic Ties Have Helped Neither Her Case Nor The Image Of Irish Travelers". *Newsweek.Com*. Updated: 29 October 2007. Accessed 17 August 2008. http://www.newsweek.com/id/65134
77   Riley, Amanda (South Carolina). "Unwanted Exposure". *Time in Partnership with CNN*. 7 October 2002 accessed 9 September 2008. http://www.time.com/time/0,8816,1003381,00.html

young married couple with very short notice. The father of the bride first contacted me and even though I had no conflict in my schedule I had to inform the father that I was unable to officiate because I was blind with cataracts.

This wedding was taking place in Memphis between two families one from the Mississippi Travelers and the other from the Georgia Travelers. It was impossible to postpone the date as many family members had already arrived from South Carolina. Within fifteen minutes of the first call, I received a second call from a different Traveler who asked me what he could do to help me out so that I could do the wedding. "We can pick you up, if you can't drive."[78] He offered.

"Father", he continued, "We really would like you to do this. The kids like you. You put them at ease."[79] The loyalty shared with the Traveler community prompted me to agree to perform the ceremony with the assistance of another ordained minister who would read parts of the service I had not committed to memory.

I personally feel this was a turning point in the relationship between the Travelers and me. Although the relationship had been respectful previously, this opened up the relationship to new dimension.

It became obvious to me that word of my blindness spread through the community as their reaction was one of kindness and caring; sharing their experiences with cataracts, offering assistance and names of doctors who could perform corrective surgery. Those who attended the wedding also expressed their gratitude.

Names and the naming of children is of importance to the family. Although there is not one formalized, accepted practice for naming a child among all of the Irish Travelers each group seems

---

78   Un-named Traveler. Telephone call. 2 January 2008
79   Un-named Traveler. Telephone call. 2 January 2008

to maintain their own traditions that reinforce the family and the family name.

In Memphis, Tennessee for example "Johnny" as opposed to John and "Jim" as opposed to James are often first names of boys. The first born son is traditionally named after the grandfathers, a practice that is not that uncommon for other Irish-Americans. Common girl names are Mary, Katie, and Bridget.

Within the Irish Traveler community there are still eight prominent surnames, representing the eight families that first emigrated from Ireland. Because a son is commonly named after their grandfather it is not uncommon to have more than one male in the community with the same first and last names. Amanda Riley mentioned "Jim (Penn) Sherlock" in her article about "Unwanted Exposure". [80] "Penn" is the nickname given to Jim Sherlock so people will know who they refer to. In Memphis, one Traveler is known as "John the Third" in order to distinguish himself from his father, grandfather or son. [81]

"John the Third" told me when outsiders criticize the way the Travelers do things, marriages, etc., he asks them, "Can you tell me the history of your family?"[82] He then proceeds to show his knowledge of his family going back several generations. "John the Third" emphasizes the strong "family values" exhibited by the Travelers because they respect and maintain a tradition which previous generation held as true.

---

80   Riley, Amanda (South Carolina). "Unwanted Exposure". *Time in Partnership with CNN*. 7 October 2002 accessed 9 September 2008. http://www.time.com/time/0,8816,1003381,00.html
81   "John the Third" has frequently been a spokesperson for the Irish Travelers in Memphis, TN. He is known by many advocates for the Travelers as the contact to the community and is highly respected.
82   John the Third. Personal Interview. 25 November 2008

Education

Dr. Mary E. Andereck not only studied the Irish Travelers in Memphis, Tennessee for her doctoral dissertation, she later became the principal at one of the Roman Catholic grade schools in Memphis. Her research reveals an interesting balance that is maintained by the Travelers in order to be compliant with truancy laws, provide their children with an education and maintain the strong traditional ties to the Traveler culture in spite of having to socialize with non-Travelers.

Formal education is not a priority for a majority of the Travelers as they feel they can better prepare and teach their children to have the skills necessary to provide for their future family. In 1998, Kathy Steele of the South Carolina bureau of the *Augusta Chronicle* wrote an article on Irish Traveler parents who were found guilty of not sending their children to school:

> AIKEN -- An Irish Traveler couple pleaded guilty Monday to failing to send their daughter to school between 1994 and 1997. Their attorney, Kelly Zier, said Pete Joseph and Rose Marie Sherlock didn't intend to violate the Compulsory School Attendance Act.
>
> They were just doing what their parents and grandparents in the Traveler community did before them. He said Mr. Sherlock, 47, completed ninth grade and Mrs. Sherlock, 41, finished sixth grade.
>
> Because of that tradition, the Sherlocks didn't believe what they did was contributing to the delinquency of a minor, which was the charge filed against them, Mr. Zier said.
>
> ``Tradition is something that's a hard thing to change,'' he said. ``They did what has been the custom of their family for all

these years. They know and understand that's not law. Law and custom must come into compliance."[83]

Andereck states, "Travelers, until the 1930's, rarely attended school."[84] Harper reported, "Some parents hired tutors for their children, but tutoring was only of short duration or just long enough for children to learn to read and write."[85]

Typically it is rare for Traveler children to complete school beyond the eighth grade.

Even though formal education is not a priority, the Traveler community does take pride when one of their own makes achievements within the educational institutions. One Traveler boasted that his son graduated from Bishop Byrne High School.[86] Pride in educational pursuits however, take a back seat to learning about the culture of the Travelers.

Andereck writes:

One Mississippi Traveler boy attended a Catholic high school for two years just to play football. Two other Mississippi Traveler boys won college football scholarships. One attended Louisiana State University and the other attended Notre Dame University. Neither returned for their second year because of low grades, but they were highly respected by the Traveler community. The respect had nothing to do with the educational achievements, however, but with the fact that the boys played football. Travelers are avid football fans and Louisiana State University and Notre Dame are their favorite teams even today

83   Steele, Kathy, South Carolina Bureau. "Couple pleaded guilty to failing to send daughter to school". *The Augusta Chronicle.* Web posted September 1, 1998. Accessed 8 August 2008. http://chronicle.augusta.com/stories/090198/met_124-1130.shtml

84   Andereck, Mary E. *Ethnic Awareness and the School: An Ethnographic Study.* Newbury Park, CA: SAGE Publications, Inc. 1992. P.35

85   Harper, Jared V. *The Irish Travelers of Georgia.* Thesis (Ph. D.)--University of Georgia, 1977, 1984. p.46 - 47

86   Un-named Traveler. Personal Interview. 25 May 2008

because of these two Traveler boys in addition to the Catholic influence on both universities as well as the Irish orientation of Notre Dame.[87]

Travelers believe their children need to know the basics of "reading, writing and arithmetic". They have made accommodations to ensure their children are provided with that knowledge often by sending them to parochial schools. Travelers believe what their children learn in the early grades will provide them with the tools they need to provide for and raise a family. Teaching and training begins at a very early age. Young boys are encouraged to join their father and uncles on the road and young girls learn how to take care of the home and care for younger siblings.

---

87   Andereck, Mary E. *Ethnic Awareness and the School: An Ethnographic Study*. Newbury Park, CA: SAGE Publications, Inc. 1992 p 35-36

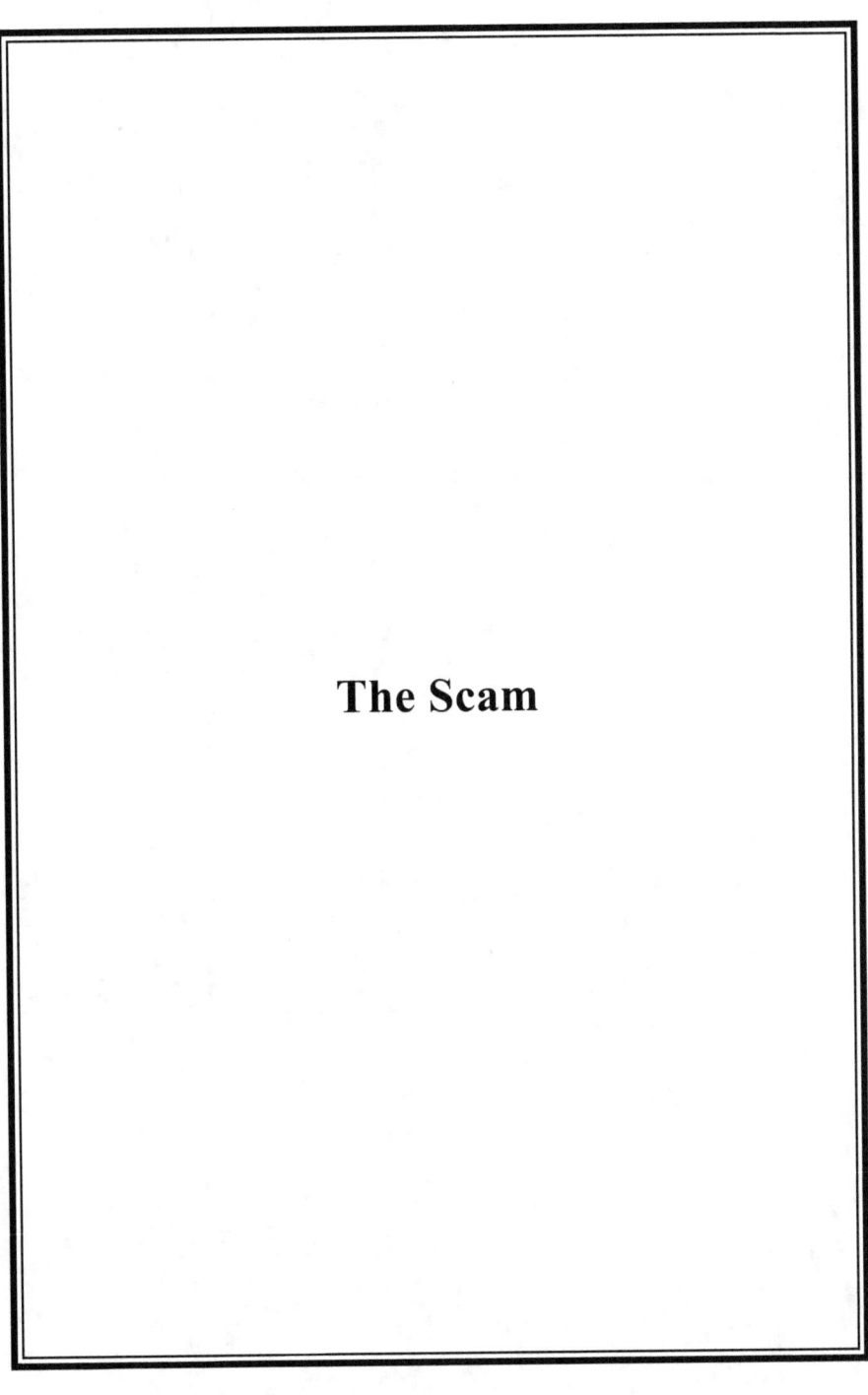

The Scam

For centuries Irish Travelers in the United States, Ireland and elsewhere have been called "scammers" and "con-men". A simple search of the Internet will quickly unveil a list of articles and public notices implicating the Irish Travelers of being involved in criminal activity.

Don Wright wrote a book, over a period of 15 years, on the "con-artist" ways of Irish Travelers. Wright, a free-lance writer, came in contact with Travelers while working for a trade magazine called *Trailer Life*. Wright calls his book *SCAM!: Inside America's Con Artist Clans (Uncovering America's most secret crime families in a true story of swindles, betrayal and murder)*, published by Cottage Publications in 1996.[88]

In his book he bases a great deal of his reporting on interviews conducted with a "Jimmy Burke", a young Irish Traveler from North Augusta, GA. (This would be the area of Murphy Village). Other details are from police reports and interviews with law enforcement agents across the United States.

Wright identifies several "traveler" groups: Irish Travelers who are grouped as "Southern Travelers" or "Georgia Travelers" based primarily out of Murphy Village, Edgefield, SC; Mississippi Travelers primarily based out of a trailer parks on Shelby Drive and Lamar Avenue in Memphis, Tennessee and "Greenhorn Travelers" or "Western Travelers" based out of White Settlement, TX (also known as Texas Travelers).

Additionally, there are Northern Travelers, who are of Irish heritage but not traditionally gathered in larger groups, as well as English Travelers and Scottish Travelers. Both of these groups

---

88   Wright, Don. *SCAM! Inside America's Con Artist Clans*. Elkhart, IN. Cottage Publications. 1996

resemble the "Irish Travelers" but are ethnically and nationally identified as different.

I begin with the reference to Wright as an example of the type of information that is available to the general public about the Travelers. Wright claims his book is non-fiction. If this is the case, one may be justifiably scared of the Irish Travelers because of the web, or network, of nefarious people that he portrays. Wright's 'truth' does not reflect actual, real-world truth and accuracy.

Lorcan "Larry" Otway, J.D., is an activist involved with several Traveler communities.[89] I initially contacted Larry Otway because of his involvement with the Madelyne Toogood case in 2002. He has been an outspoken defender of the Traveler community and culture to the national Press. Otway presented a paper on the "Racialization of Irish Travellers in America" which he delivered at Trinity College Law School.

Otway stated, "There is among other things in the paper, an analysis of the book *Scam* in its factual inaccuracies, and the author's lack of credentials or credibility." Otway continued writing, "Most of the writing about the Traveller community, and the Romany community is done, either by sensationalist press, authors without credentials, or the police."[90]

Arthur F. Kinney authored a chapter in *Rogues and Early Modern English Culture,* entitled "Afterword, (Re) presenting the

---

89   Locan "Larry" Otway of New York, NY has a law degree and has worked as an activist for Traveler communities and other marginalized people and groups of people for many years. As a "political scientist, Otway has studied the Travelers and fought for their rights since the 1970's". according to Sheila Flynn of The South Bend Tribune in an article published on the Internet entitled "*Irish Travellers: Media coverage racist, unresearched*' posted 8 October 2002 accessed 7 August 2008. Otway also publishes a blog: *Plain in the City* on http://plaininthecity.blogspot.com/.

90   Stygles, John M. "Pavee folks…"Irish Travellers". E-mail from Lorcan "Larry" Otway. 31 August 2008

Early Modern Rogue" in which he compared the Travelers to the "Tutors and Stuarts" in rogue literature. Kinney states: [91]

> They arrange their children's marriages, speak their own "canting tongue," a strange Gaelic-English dialect in which *Misli shayjo* means "Go away, the police are here!" and are accused by outsiders as con artists who cheat the elderly by overcharging them or by performing faulty work.[92]

> Their rules (Tutor's and Stuart's), like the practices of the Irish Travelers, are designed to keep them together, sharing with one another, and to keep them apart, independent of those constituting the larger society. Membership in the Irish Traveler communities, as in Dekker's fraternities of vagabonds, is clearly delineated and clearly defined, underwritten and confirmed by social and linguistic practices.[93]

Otway touches upon a problem that became apparent during this research; most positive things said about the Traveler community have come from academia. Kinney illustrates how the mystique of a group lends itself to literary license. This does not mean scholars are naive and have closed their eyes to unscrupulous acts, but it does present a challenge in understanding the true nature of this community.

The primary sources of information to the general public on the Travelers appear in the newspapers or on television. The following is a typical example of what the public might hear on television:

---

91   Kinney, Arthur E. *Afterword, (Re)presenting the Early Modern Rogue.* Dionne, Craig, and Steve Mentz, Editors. *Rogues and Early Modern English Culture.* Ann Arbor: University of Michigan Press, 2004.

92   Kinney, Arthur E. *Afterword, (Re)presenting the Early Modern Rogue.* Dionne, Craig, and Steve Mentz, Editors. *Rogues and Early Modern English Culture.* Ann Arbor: University of Michigan Press, 2004. P.361

93   Kinney, Arthur E. *Afterword, (Re)presenting the Early Modern Rogue.* Dionne, Craig, and Steve Mentz, Editors. *Rogues and Early Modern English Culture.* Ann Arbor: University of Michigan Press, 2004. P. 362

"Irish Traveler Behind Bars" reported by *WTAP News* on November 2, 2005.

A 48-year-old Irish traveler was brought from Indiana to Wood County Wednesday to face charges relating to a senior citizen scam. Jimmy Riley just got out of prison in Indiana and Wednesday night he was put in the North Central Regional Jail on $25,000 bond. Parkersburg police say Riley is responsible for passing himself off as a handyman to an 85-year-old woman, then having an accomplice ransack her home. The crime happened in July. The arrest is being attributed to a story we aired on *WTAP-TV*.

"Through that interview and that story on TV as well as the internet, law enforcement in the state of South Carolina picked up on that and contacted us and with their help we were able to narrow our investigation," says Detective Greg Nangle. Nangle says other arrests are pending. Irish travelers are basically traveling scam artists who prey on senior citizens.[94]

The above was the copy used by Denise Alex who reported this story. Larry Otway is quoted above stating: "Most of the writing about the Traveller community, and the Romany community is done, either by sensationalist press, authors without credentials, or the police."[95]

The statement read by the reporter, "Irish travelers are basically traveling scam artists who prey on senior citizens,"[96] has no basis what-so-ever and is typical according to Otway's statements.

---

94   Alex, Denise. "Irish Traveler Behind Bars". *WTAP-TV News*. Indiana. Posted 3 November 2005. Accessed 30 June 2008. http://www.wtap.com/news/headlines/1944332.html

95   Stygles, John M. "Pavee folks…"Irish Travellers". E-mail from Lorcan "Larry" Otway. 31 August 2008

96   Alex, Denise. "Irish Traveler Behind Bars". *WTAP-TV News*. Indiana. Posted 3 November 2005. Accessed 30 June 2008. http://www.wtap.com/news/headlines/1944332.html

Is accuracy the reporter's motivation or is there some other agenda? November, the time of this report, is typically "sweeps ratings" month for local television.[97] There is a trend in newsrooms to produce tabloid-styled sensational stories to help increase ratings. The truth is often a casualty in the pursuit of ratings.

For most Americans their first knowledge of this community of people called Irish Travelers occurred on the days following September 13, 2002 when Madelyne Toogood was videotaped in a Kohl's shopping center parking lot hitting her daughter in the back seat of their SUV. The reaction of the media and many Americans was a sincere reaction to what appeared to be a child repeatedly hit by an adult.

The actions of Ms. Toogood stirred emotions and the public reaction was hostile. When Toogood was arrested she revealed she was an Irish Traveler and that just added to the sensationalism relating to the story.

In a *Newsweek* report posted on the Internet the writers' state:

When Madelyne Toogood stepped before the TV cameras last week and tearfully admitted to beating her four-year-old daughter, she also turned the spotlight onto a group of people that had gone largely unnoticed in the United States for more than a century, and liked it that way.

---

97   "Sweeps are designated months during the year when Nielsen Media Research measures all local markets. We survey the majority of our 210 local television markets in November, February, May and July (Local People Meter markets, however, are measured 365 days a year). These months are known as "sweep" months, and the data are used by local stations and cable systems to set local advertising rates and to make program decisions. The term "sweep" originated in the 1950s, when Nielsen Media Research mailed and processed diaries to sample households, starting with the East Coast and "sweeping" across the nation."
Source: "FAQ TV Ratings. *Nielsen Media Research*. 2009. Accessed 25 January 2009 http://www.nielsenmedia.com/nc/portal/site/Public/menuitem.55dc65b4a7d5adff3f65936147a062a0/?vgnextoid=34953b318b906010VgnVCM100000880a260aRCRD.

In her televised appearances, the 25-year-old mother of three confirmed that she is a member of the Irish Travelers, nomadic descendents of immigrants who fled to the United States during the mid-19th century to escape the potato famine. Until now, few Americans had even heard of the group; those who had associated the Travelers with home-repair scams reported in their local press.[98]

In my discussions with Larry Otway he wrote:

"The Madeline Toogood case is a good one for seeing the treatment of Travellers. It was, in fact, a case about racial profiling. The court quickly found her to be a very good mother, with a good network of family help. Her mother was not literate, but raised her to be a good reader and articulate. She availed herself of programs for nomadic people in Texas, so that her children went a step beyond her generation, attending school and doing well in that."[99]

As a result of that incident, Toogood received a year's probation and a $500 fine. The more serious charges against her were dismissed, despite all the media attention.[100]

Yet, it is not just the press that circulates blanket statements about the Irish Travelers. The Governor's Office of Consumer Affairs in Georgia issued this press release on May 14, 2007:

98   Newsweek Web Exclusive. "Seriously Prejudiced: Madelyne Toogood's Ethnic Ties Have Helped Neither Her Case Nor The Image Of Irish Travelers". *Newsweek*. Updated 29 October 2007. Accessed 17 August 2008. http://www.newsweek.com/id/65134
99   Stygles, John M. "Pavee folks…"Irish Travellers". E-mail from Lorcan "Larry" Otway. 31 August 2008
100   National Briefing | Midwest: Indiana: "Sentence In Videotaped Hitting". New York Times.Com. February 15, 2003. Accessed May 8, 2009. (A version of this article appeared in print on Saturday, February 15, 2003, on section A page 16 of the New York edition.) http://www.nytimes.com/2003/02/15/us/national-briefing-midwest-indiana-sentence-in-videotaped hitting. html?n=Top/Reference/Times Topics/Subjects/P/Probation%20and%20Parole

Irish Travelers Perpetuate a Tradition of Fraud

Around the time that schools let out, individuals known as Irish Travelers load up their pick-up trucks and take their show on the road. Sadly, their business is not a very entertaining one and can cost you way more than a ticket to the Big Top. These descendants of Irish immigrants live in nomadic clans and make their living by perpetrating home improvement fraud and selling substandard machinery at huge mark-ups.

While there are several communities of Irish travelers throughout the South, the largest is an enclave located just outside North Augusta, South Carolina. With the exception of their "marks", Travelers have little contact with outsiders. Generally, in the spring, they spread out throughout the eastern seaboard and beyond.

Travelers go door-to-door, often targeting the elderly. They usually drive unmarked pick-up trucks with out-of-state plates, often from South Carolina. They are pavers, roofers, painters, [and] repairmen who just happen to have left-over materials from a previous job, allowing them to offer huge discounts, but only if you act now. You will rarely receive a written contract from them, and if you do, the contact information will have only a toll-free number and a post office box, making it impossible to track down the conman when the homeowner discovers the inferior quality of the workmanship and materials.[101]

The Consumer Affairs office then offers a list of suggestions helpful for selecting someone who does home-improvements. Yet, the impact of this press release is that it has been issued from a place of authority. The press release implies "all" Irish Travelers participate in fraud and confidence games. With such an authoritative source,

---

101   Cloud, Bill. "Irish Travelers Perpetuate a Tradition of Fraud". *State of Georgia: Governor's Office of Consumer Affairs.* 14 May 2007. 7 August 2008. http://www.georgia.gov/00/press_print/0,2669,5426814_94800056_94847127,00.html

newspapers like *The Weekly* go ahead and print the press release without any changes.[102]

While a doctoral candidate in anthropology at the University of Pittsburg, Alan Katruska studied the Irish Travelers "centered mainly on interactions with the settled world and conflict between groups."[103] Katruska created a website, now archived, to aid the public, especially the press in gleaning a better understanding of this culture.[104]

Katruska believes, "The No. 1 misconception is that all Travelers are criminals," he says. "It's just one of the aspects of stereotype creation where people are all viewed as being the same because they are part of a group, and when news of a person behaving in a certain way comes out, people think everyone is like that."[105]

Interviews conducted with members of the Mississippi Travelers provide a different viewpoint than most of the media and law enforcement. When direct questions were asked about the "image" of being scammers, a sense of frustration, and defensiveness prevailed. Initially members of the group avoided the topic and stressed the more positive aspects of the community and what they feel makes them better than most people in today's society. They emphasized their close ties with family and tradition, a deep responsibility in taking care of their elderly, and love of children. They focused on saying, "we don't go looking for trouble."[106]

---

102   "Irish Travelers Perpetuate a Tradition of Fraud". *The Weekly: Your Neighborhood Newspaper.* 14 May 2007.
28 August 2008. http://www.theweekly.com/news/2007/May/14/Irish_Travelers.html
103   Stygles, John M. "Irish Travellers". E-mail from Alan Katruska. 1 October 2008
104   Irish Traveler website created by Alan Katruska: http://web.archive.org/web/20040925082925/http://www.pitt.edu/~alkst3/Traveller.html
105   Newsweek Web Exclusive. "Seriously Prejudiced: Madelyne Toogood's Ethnic Ties Have Helped Neither Her Case Nor The Image Of Irish Travelers". *Newsweek.* Updated 29 October 2007. Accessed 17 August 2008. http://www.newsweek.com/id/65134
106   Un-named Traveler. Personal Interview. 23 December 2008

Travelers are acutely aware of the negative image that has been perpetuated upon them. They emphasize the fact that the majority of Travelers are independent business persons who, when working, deal with the public to provide various services. They stress that the number of complaints received about dissatisfaction of work quality or price is typical in any business, especially home-improvement. They also emphasized they work diligently to resolve these concerns.

One Traveler did admit, "There are some people who are of a Traveler group, or because they make a living on the road are considered Travelers. Some do try to take advantage of people," expressed one Traveler. "But they don't belong to this community."[107]

This Traveler was adamant about this topic, he continued:

Because of this negative image that police have about any home-improvement folks from out-of-state, we are bound to get caught up in the web of accusations and name-calling. Occasionally we might be stopped, or one of our customers will after-the-fact complain about the price of the job, but we do what it takes to keep them happy. We don't want to get in trouble with the law.

What usually happens is we will negotiate a price to do a job upfront. When the customer agrees, we do the job, then a few days later that customer gets to talking with neighbors, family or friends and they say, "you could have had that done for cheaper..." and then they complain. Everyone always knows of a better deal, but we get holding the bag for their complaint of either 'the work wasn't good enough' or 'you charged me too much'.

The fact that we discuss the cost upfront and it was agreed to apparently doesn't matter. If they complain to the cops, we could go to jail and then all our workers are out of work, so we

---

107   Ibid.

just settle the matter. Sometimes I wonder if we're the ones being played.[108]

Another Traveler expressed the scam in this way:

The problem is because of all the bad stuff that's been said about the Travelers, people think they have an advantage over us. We're just trying to make a living like everyone else.

….sure, sometimes, you know if a job cost say 500 bucks and you can sell it for 2000 you try to make the profit, but they agree to the price up front. Then what happens is someone might be a talking to them and they say, "You paid how much?" and they start questioning what they did. That's when they start to complain. If they [thought] the job was expensive they would not have accepted it at that price.

If they had said, "Oh, 2000 is too much," I'd probably have come back with, "Well let me look it over and see what I can do…" and then maybe suggested a lesser price. It's all about compromise and bargaining.

You see if I make an agreement with you and you say ok then that's the agreement. If I tell you it's going to cost one thing and then say it is going to cost more, then that's not the way to do business. But if I start the job, painting you know, and find out that the wood or surface needs to be replaced, that is probably going to change the price.

I always let the people know if I have a problem like that. I even show them why.[109]

These statements are the positions of individual Travelers who claim to be regular business persons trying to earn a living and not "scammers" who commit fraudulent acts.

In their book: *To Steal, Traveling Con Artists, Their Games, Their Rules---Your Money,* Dennis Marlock and John Dowling

---

108   Un-named Traveler. Personal Interview. 23 December 2008
109   Un-named Traveler. Personal Interview. 25 November 2008

devote a chapter to the Irish Travelers. The authors looked at the Traveler's profession of faith in the Catholic Church saying:

"Travelers have a long tradition, a rigid set of morals, and a way of life that has been handed down from their ancestors…the Travelers have a dual set of ethics, one set for dealing with other Travelers and a second for relating to country folk [non-Traveler]. While a traveler may not ethically exploit others of his own kind, any relatively safe exploitation of country folk is a legitimate and, in fact, highly laudable."[110]

There is a distinct dichotomy between what Travelers claim and what non-Travelers claim. This could relate to what Marlock and Dowling suggests as a "dual set of ethics", but it may be something further, something that may become blatantly obvious when looking at the total and not just a portion of information.

The amount of negative publicity about Travelers must be reviewed and just as one would read to understand the "behind the text" implications, one must accept that there may be some truth to what is being portrayed. To use the expression, "where there's smoke, there's fire" is not an acceptance of that implication, but rather a realization that there may be a small kernel of truth to the image portrayed.

Dr. Mary E. Andereck stated in an interview with the *Commercial Appeal*, "I don't think there's even an attempt to improve their image in the United States, because I don't think they worry about it. There's no real stigma or feeling of prejudice or discrimination against them as an entire group, the way there is in Ireland. … Mississippi Travelers are middle-class people."[111]

---

110   Marlock, Dennis and John Dowling. *License to Steal: Traveling Con Artists: Their Games, Their Rules – Your Money.* Boulder, CO: Paladin Press, 1994. P. 241

111   Watson, Mark. "Mississippi Travelers: Local group settling down". *Commercial Appeal.Com.* Memphis, TN. Scripps Newspaper Group – Online. Posted 29 July 2007. Accessed 9 September 2008. http://m.commercialappeal.

In May of 2002, the United States Senate - Special Committee on Aging held hearings called: *Schemer, Scammers, and Sweetheart Deals: Financial Predators of the Elderly.* Senator John Breaux of Louisiana opened the Hearing and included in his statement the following:

> Today, we will hear a sampling of these cases involving family, home repairmen, and professional criminal groups such as Travelers and Rom Gypsies that target the elderly. On this issue, let me say up front that it is not our intent to condemn all people who consider themselves Travelers or Rom Gypsies, but to focus on those within these groups where illegal activities are the main fuel for their existence.[112]

As part of this hearing one witness, Justin White, testified that he was an "ex-Traveler from the Northwest."[113] White, who was serving a ten-year term in Idaho State Prison, told the Senators that he was born into this "way-of-life."[114] He proceeded to tell of his hardships in life, the lack of education and ways he states the Travelers rip-off people. Towards the end of the Hearing, the Chairman, Senator John Breaux, had the following exchange with Mr. White:

> The Chairman: You never finished high school?
> Mr. White: No, sir.
>
> The Chairman: You never went to grammar school?
> Mr. White: No, sir
>
> The Chairman: In a way you are a victim, are you not?

com/news/2007/Jul/29/nomads-of-ireland/

112   United States Congress. Senate Special Committee on Aging. *Schemer, Scammers, and Sweetheart Deals: Financial Predators of the Elderly.* 107th Congress Second Session. S. Hearing 107-581. Washington: GPO, 2002. http://bulk.resource.org/gpo.gov/hearings/107s/80873.txt published 2002. accessed 12 September 2008

113   Ibid.
114   Ibid.

Mr. White: Well, yeah, you might put it that way.

The Chairman: Well, we appreciate you being here. I mean obviously you have done a great deal of damage to a large number of people, but hopefully your story can help enlighten a lot of people about the problems that are out there and for that we thank you for being with us.[115]

Justin White, like Jimmy Burke, who is the main character in *SCAM!*, used the opportunity of having a public forum to tell people what they wanted to hear. Justin White was a convicted criminal yet he was able to convince the Senator that it was he who was a victim. A closer reading into *SCAM!* and the hearings transcripts reveal contradictions and creative expressionism.

White stated he was an ex-Traveler, yet even Travelers who marry non-Travelers, and may be shunned for that association outside the community; are still considered Travelers unless they do something to discredit the community.[116] If he was in fact an ex-Traveler he must have been "kicked-out" of the group of which he was associated.

Don Wright author of *SCAM!* quotes a Traveler saying: "Jimmy Burke was a pathological liar. Nobody had anything to do with him because he was a low-life."[117]

"The Burkes, she said, "are not real Travelers" because their mother was a non-Traveler. The Burke children, she added, "Were not raise, they were drug up. And when they were fifteen years old, they were told to leave."[118]

Max J. Skidmore, a professor of political science and American studies at the University of Missouri-Kansas City wrote in an article for the *Journal of American Culture* that focused on the culture of

115   Ibid.
116   Un-named Traveler. Personal Interview. 1 December 2008
117   Wright, Don. *SCAM! Inside America's Con Artist Clans*. Elkhart, IN. Cottage Publications. 1996. P.476
118   Ibid.

Travelers. His focus was on a group or clan known as the "Williamson Travelers" based in Cincinnati, Ohio.[119] The Williamson's are also known as Northern Travelers. "[They] are descendants of Irish, Scottish, and English nomadic tinkers, "Travelers," who are a staunchly Protestant as the Gypsies are Catholic."[120]

SCAM! author Don Wright stated Jimmy Burke was a member of the Northern Travelers.[121] If the Senate Hearing testimony of Justin White is to be believed he was not a member of the Irish Travelers from Texas, Tennessee-Memphis, or South Carolina-Georgia and was possibly a member of the Northern Travelers.

While there are differences, as one discovers, between the Northern Travelers and other Traveler groups, there are also some similarities. Skidmore offers one similarity: "the Travelers do practice "family values" to an extent that any member of Congress would have to praise. Their commitment to Bible study and their reservations about public schooling suggest something in common with many members of the Christian Coalition."[122]

---

119   Skidmore, Max J. "The folk culture of 'the travelers': clans of con artist." *Journal of American Culture*. 20.3 (Fall 1997): p.73. http://newfirstsearch. oclc.org/images/WSPL/wsppdfl/HTML/02583/KG70H/HSN.HTM accessed 10/12/2008
120   Ibid. P.74
121   Wright, Don. SCAM! *Inside America's Con Artist Clans*. Elkhart, IN. Cottage Publications. 1996. P266
122   Skidmore, Max J. "The folk culture of 'the travelers': clans of con artist." *Journal of American Culture*. 20.3 (Fall 1997): p.80. http://newfirstsearch. oclc.org/images/WSPL/wsppdfl/HTML/02583/KG70H/HSN.HTM accessed 10/12/2008

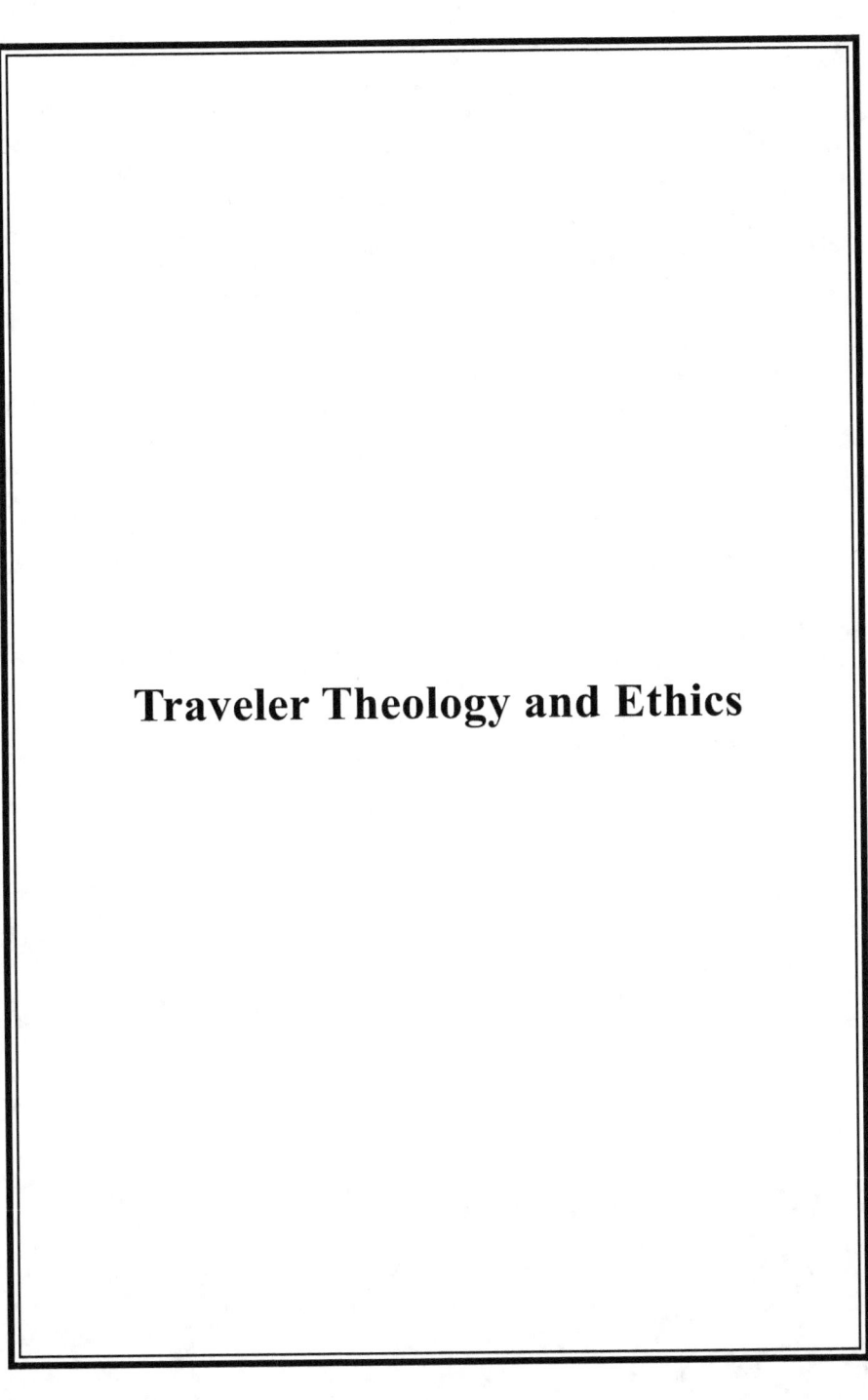

Traveler Theology and Ethics

When we look at the Irish Traveler community and seek to understand their theology and ethics, one begins to develop or understand their particular worldview; or what Garth Kasimu Baker-Fletcher refers to as the "Cultural Logics" of the person or group.[123] Each culture has a distinctive way of thinking, a way of seeing life that they pass on to their children. This is the reality shared in common by the group and it is what distinguishes them from other ethnic groups, or cultures. It is what distinguishes them from what a majority society would see as consistent with their norms and mores.

Part of what shapes the "cultural logics are those structured and institutionalized understandings that shape our political, religious, economic, and intellectual viewpoints."[124] Baker-Fletcher states: "ethical categories of loyalties, values, and norms arise in direct connection to one's cultural logics."[125]

Marlock and Dowling, authors of *License to Steal: Traveling Con Artists: Their Games, Their Rules – Your Money,* raised the question of the Irish Travelers having a "dual set of ethics." When trying to plot out and analyze the components that qualify for evaluating the Christian ethics of the Travelers one clearly sees a dualism in their cultural logics; one that is expressed within the community of Travelers and one that governs their interactions outside the group. This dualism is what one might think of as a set behaviors or habits expressed at home and a different set of behaviors and habits expressed in public. An example might be of a pious, highly-respected husband who abuses his family behind closed doors.

---

123   Baker-Fletcher, Garth Kasimu. *Dirty Hands: Christian Etichs in a Morally Ambiguous World.* Minneapolis: Fortress Press. 2000. P. 11
124   Ibid.
125   Ibid. p.12

What we find is a culture that prefers to remain insular in order to protect their way-of-life. They do believe they are different, special and maybe better than non-Travelers, yet they are fearful that exposure outside their community through socialization at school or where they live could adversely impact the sanctity and peace within the community.

Within the community one finds individuals who profess their faith in the Roman Catholic Church and exercise that faith through the practice of devotionals, going to Mass, receiving the Sacraments and praying to God, either directly or through Intercessors (Saints).

They believe God takes care of them because they ask for that assistance. They are good stewards in their contributions to the church as this is believed to be a way to show thanks to God.

Due to the itinerant nature of their culture, involvement in the church had traditionally been as participants at Mass and the process of receiving Sacraments. Yet, today because of a semi-settled lifestyle, and an openness of the Roman Catholic Church for lay involvement, many Traveler women are actively involved as Readers, Lectures, and Eucharistic Ministers.

The costs of maintaining the Traveler lifestyle means restricting access to outside influences. It has been suggested that one way of preventing their youth from leaving their community and adopting a different worldview is to continue the practice of marriages among young Travelers. In the State of Tennessee a youth under the age of sixteen can be married but a waiver must be issued from Juvenile Court.[126] This is a common practice of which the Travelers take advantage.

---

126   State of Tennessee Code: 36-3-107. Waiver of age requirements and waiting period. -(a) (1) (A) Except as provided in subdivision (a)(1)(B), upon good cause, the judge of the probate, juvenile, circuit or chancery court, or county mayor, shall have the power to suspend the three-day period prescribed in § 36-3-104 or in such person's judgment remove the restriction as to age herein set out, and to authorize the county clerk to issue a marriage license regardless of the waiting period or age limit.

The Roman Catholic Church in Memphis, Tennessee, does not perform the rite of marriage for any person under the age of sixteen so some Traveler families have made accommodations to their practice of faith in order to have a church ceremony. This is a breaking of the rules set locally by the church, but not only is it readily accepted by the Traveler, the church is complicit in the renting of the sanctuary to them for the ceremony. Making this type of accommodation is seen as doing the right thing for the community whose ultimate goal is to maintain the strength, unity, and continuity of the community.

Understanding where one belongs within the community is as simple as gender. To be male means to be a good provider, learn the skills of the trade, get married and support a family; then teach your son(s) the ways of the Travelers. For a female it is to learn how to take care of a household, pray, get married and have children then teach those children the ways of the Travelers. These roles may be seen as old-fashioned, yet they are considered a component of the traditional values system.

Within the community, right and wrong, good and bad is controlled by the local norms of the Travelers. In most cases, families live in direct proximity to one another. The community watches over all, and because so many are part of each other's extended family, any young people getting out of hand are quickly reigned in.

Travelers recognize that they are "sinners" just like most Christians, but they believe they have an advantage in being Roman Catholic. Traveler men especially recognize the benefits of going to Confession. There is a sense of relief received and expressed when the priest absolves them of their sins. This act makes all things better, one Traveler expressed to me.

No matter how devout in their practice of faith, the grace received from going to Confession means forgiveness. One Traveler told me that no matter what he may have done on the road, any mistakes or wrong-doings would be forgiven if he confessed to a priest.[127] Of course, this is what the Roman Catholic Church teaches.

The women of the community hold their families together in matters of faith. This is part of their mission to ensure a solid Catholic background for the children. A majority of the women are true examples of how to be a devout Roman Catholic, in their prayers and involvement with the church. The women also have a positive influence on the men of the community, whether husbands, brothers or sons.

Outside the community, when the Traveler men go about their business they lack that direct influence from their wives and mothers. The women know that the men need to go and earn a living. They worry about the dangers on the road and the conflicts they may get into. The men focus on their work and making as much money as they can.

This is where one may see a different set of ethics taking place, when the men are doing business away from their home base. The Travelers that I interviewed are adamant about the fact that the scams and confidence games that people hear about do not concern them. One Traveler informed me that it's not their group that gets into trouble. He insisted that there are only a few people that try to take advantage of people, "but when you try to cheat your way towards making a living, you always come up short."[128]

If one accepts the negative image given to the Travelers then one might have to believe there is a "dual set of ethics", yet that is still accepting a "broad-brush" approach to this community of Irish Travelers. There are several groups across United States and Canada who either claim the name of Traveler or are called Travelers because they are itinerant workers. It would be wrong to lump all groups in one category and call them scammers and confidence people.

---

127   Un-named Traveler. Personal Interview. 12 December 2008.
128   Un-named Traveler. Personal Interview. 23 November 2008

It would also be irresponsible to chastise a whole group of people because of an individual member of that group or individuals associated with related groups who may not operate their business dealings in an ethical manner.

What I can pronounce with certitude is that the people I have met, observed and interviewed are part of the Irish Traveler community, known as the Mississippi Travelers, and are people who have a keen sense of moral responsibility to their families, church and community.

The desire of these people to maintain their traditions and culture is an intentional one. As with many other intentional communities: religious orders, the Amish, and the Mennonites; the Travelers' quest for privacy is considered being secretive. In this era of transparency, society wants to know everything and if they do not have access society believes something is wrong or even nefarious.

Regardless of their intentional community status, as a whole, they express a Christian ethic that is common among traditional, ethnic Roman Catholics; a blending of good and bad within their contextual theology.

Roman Catholics are reminded every time when they enter a church of the suffering of Jesus Christ. The Traveler women relate to this suffering and the self-sacrifice. The teachings of the Roman Catholic Church are essential in the development of the ethics amongst Travelers.

Since the late 1840's, Irish Travelers have accepted the burdens that come with maintaining a culture and traditional ways. They realize that as an insular community they subject themselves to unwanted scrutiny and ridicule and this has opened them up to charges of being con artist and scammers. Yet they are willing to accept that in order to maintain what is the life-affirming dynamics of community.

So to answer the question posed within this thesis of how the Travelers justify the scam it is my position that much of the "scam" is created by prejudice and the insularity of the community. Travelers have had a long history in Ireland of being less than scrupulous and that has been carried forward by tales and folklore. Emigrating from Ireland might have provided new economic opportunities to the Travelers, yet the distance did not do anything to change the perception of those who think they know this community.

It is the insular world and the worldview of the Travelers that has given rise to this prejudice, especially the broad brushing of the community as scammers and con artists, but the reality is these are hard working people have strong family values and a deep devotion to God and the Roman Catholic Church. Their Christian ethic is based in the foundation of the teachings of the Roman Catholic Church.

The Travelers are a community of people who continue to find security and protection within a culture and traditional way of living. They are gregarious and enjoy life and this is often confused with being sly – because they are too happy. Their life is a simple one. Their values are basic. Their faith is strong. Their loyalty and allegiances are to a community they know will continue to support them as long as they are able to maintain and instill the traditions, values and culture on each successive generation.

Traveler women seriously believe that any negative talk about them, as a group, is just another cross they have to bear. The women tend to be the moral compasses outside of the church and reflect this through the virtues of faith, love and hope. These "theological virtues" are most noticeable in the effort they exercise in raising of their children.

The way Traveler women hear and understand stories like the Syro-Phoenician woman in Matthew 15:21-28 is way of expressing that their faith too can overcome any obstacles of un-worthiness, and in the course of things teach us about what it means to be a good person.

Experience and tradition along with the moral teachings of the Roman Catholic Church (Scripture) all work with Reason in the formation of Christian ethics of the Irish Travelers.

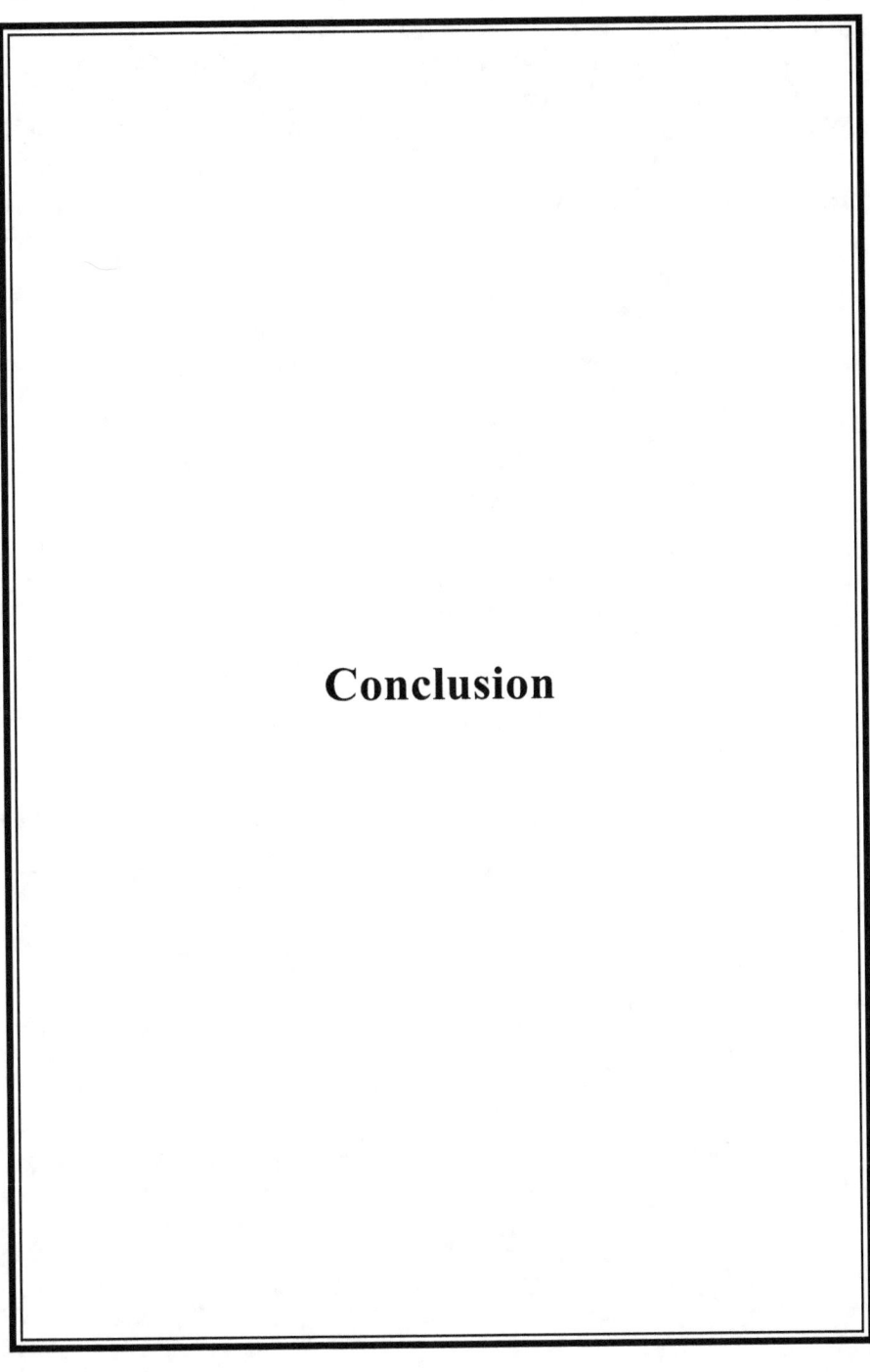

Conclusion

When I began this research I sought to understand the contextual theology and ethics of the Irish Travelers and how they justified the scam. I asked this question assuming what I had heard, read, and seen regarding the Irish Travelers was true. Yet, what I discovered was quite different.

There is a disconnect between what is known about the Irish Travelers and what is a more accurate or balanced view of life within the Traveler community. While reading news articles and internet blogs concerning the Travelers one comment kept reappearing, I paraphrase: "and they're supposed to be devout Roman Catholics". Whether addressing the Madelyn Toogood incident or some home improvement scam, outsiders (non-Travelers) felt justified in saying the Travelers show no moral scruples in their daily life despite the appearance of being faithful Roman Catholics.

For non-Travelers the only truth they may know about the Irish Travelers is their connection to the Roman Catholic Church and their devout faith. Yet, some non-Travelers will use this one truth to spin a web of nefarious allegations and myths in the attempt to convince others that this is a group of people that should not be trusted.

The Irish Travelers have made an intentional choice to maintain their traditions and live within a community holding true to a common vision and way of life. They are secure and comfortable within this community, and they maintain this way of life by excluding outsiders. Outsiders see this intentional community as not wanting to assimilate with the rest of society and conform to ociety's standards which spur speculation into what actually goes on within the Traveler community.

The Irish Traveler's choice of an intentional community is no different than the choice made by The Amish, Mennonites, or cloistered Benedictine Monks. The devotion to the Roman Catholic

Church as portrayed by the Travelers is the glue that holds their community together. It is their moral and ethical standard.

Within the Traveler community one sees a strong moral ethic in the interactions between families and individuals. There is a "code of honor – shame" within this community. There are expectations within the community that guide their way of life. One is expected to function within the community for the betterment of all. To dishonor the community by acting out, being disloyal or abusive is responded to in an adverse manner by the community. It is recognized that the survival of the community rests in everyone sharing a common interest in its survival.

Outside the community, the interactions with non-Travelers tends to be on a business level. A majority of Travelers are self-employed and earn a living within the home improvement business. This occupational choice adds to the myths and allegations made against Travelers.

According to the United States Better Business Bureau, "Many homeowners feel that finding a trustworthy contractor is a difficult task. According to the […] BBB/Gallup Trust in Business Survey, 73 percent of respondents indicated that they didn't have a great deal or a lot of trust in contractors."[129] This opinion poll did not single out the Travelers when respondents were questioned; it concerned questions of trust relating to all home improvement contractors.

A lack of confidence due to a lack of knowledge by homeowners can cause one to question the cost and quality of work for repairs they have contracted. Oft times Travelers are easy targets because they are itinerant workers and they belong to a closed community. Prejudice exhibited by law enforcement and media contribute to their being singled out and unjustly identified as "scammers."

---

129   Better Business Bureau. *BBB Advice on Hiring Contractors for Home Improvements and Remodeling*. http://www.bbb.org/us/article/4948. 5/1/2008 accessed 5/12/2009

Just as I have tried to state that broad brushing this community with the label of scammers or con artists is unjust, I can also state that within any community or group there may be exceptions. It would be naive to state that all people are 100% honorable in the same way I would not say that 100% of people are dishonorable. But categorizing all Travelers as being unethical and immoral is prejudicial and discriminatory.

The key to understanding this community is through knowledge and that knowledge is received through access to the community. The community limits access to outsiders, even those with the best of intentions, because too much exposure can rob them of their way of life. This may be one of the reasons Travelers do not confute negative and prejudicial articles, books and media reports.

Since the 1970's only a handful of scholars have conducted any type of research on the Irish Travelers. Of that research most have focused within the disciplines of Anthropology, Sociology and Education. This thesis is a first to approach a study of the Irish Travelers from a theology and Christian ethics discipline and I believe will contribute to a better understanding of the community.

Further study and research of this community is necessary for academia and the Traveler community as a whole. It is important that the Traveler community has knowledgeable and sympathetic advocates who recognize that their way of life is their choice and that choice needs to be defended.

Bibliography

Ahearn, David Oki, and Peter R. Gathje. <u>Doing Right and Being Good: Catholic and Protestant Readings in Christian Ethics</u>. Collegeville, Minn: Liturgical Press, 2005.

Andereck, Mary E. <u>Ethnic Awareness and the School: An Ethnographic Study</u>. Newbury Park, CA: SAGE Publications, Inc. 1992.

Baker-Fletcher, Garth Kasimu. <u>Dirty Hands: Christian Etichs in a Morally Ambiguous World.</u> Minneapolis: Fortress Press. 2000.

Coogan, Tim Pat. <u>Wherever Green Is Worn: The Story of the Irish Diaspora</u>. London: Hutchinson, 2001.

Hardcastle, David A., Patricia R. Powers, and Stanley Wenocur. <u>Community Practice Theories and Skills for Social Workers</u>. Oxford: Oxford University Press, 2004

Harper, Jared V. <u>The Irish Travelers of Georgia</u>. Thesis (Ph. D.)-- University of Georgia, 1977, 1984.

Kinney, Arthur E. *Afterword, (Re)presenting the Early Modern Rogue*. Dionne, Craig, and Steve Mentz, Editors. <u>Rogues and Early Modern English Culture</u>. Ann Arbor: University of Michigan Press, 2004.

McCaffrey, Lawrence John. <u>Textures of Irish America</u>. Syracuse, N.Y.: Syracuse University Press, 1992.

Marlock, Dennis and John Dowling. <u>License to Steal: Traveling Con Artists: Their Games, Their Rules – Your Money.</u> Boulder, CO: Paladin Press, 1994

Miller, Kerby A. <u>Emigrants and Exiles: Ireland and the Irish Exodus to North America</u>. New York: Oxford University Press, 1985.

Quinlan, Kieran. <u>Strange Kin: Ireland and the American South</u>. Baton Rouge: Louisiana State University Press, 2005.

Sedmak, Clemens, <u>Doing Local Theology: A Guide for Artisians of a New Humanity.</u> Maryknoll: Orbis Books. 2007

Skidmore, Max J. "The folk culture of 'the travelers': clans of con artist." <u>Journal of American Culture</u>. 20.3 (Fall 1997): 73-80. http:// newfirstsearch.oclc.org/images/ WSPL/wsppdf1/HTML/02583/KG70H/ HSN.HTM accessed 10/12/2008

Whitney, Kim Ablon. <u>See You Down The Road.</u> New York._Dell Laurel-Leaf/Random House. 2004

Wright, Don. <u>SCAM! Inside America's Con Artist Clans</u>. Elkhart, IN. Cottage Publications. 1996

www.ingramcontent.com/pod-product-compliance
Lightning Source LLC
Chambersburg PA
CBHW062051280526
45788CB00003B/1185